We Should Look To Our Moat

by

Vice Admiral Sir Louis Le Bailly KBE, CB, DL,
Hon DSc(Plymouth)C.Eng, F.I.Mech E, F.I.MarEst, F.I.PET

Order this book online at www.trafford.com/07-2029
or email orders@trafford.com

Most Trafford titles are also available at major online book retailers.

Note for Librarians: A cataloguing record for this book is available from Library and Archives Canada at www.collectionscanada.ca/amicus/index-e.html

ISBN: 978-1-4251-4726-6

We at Trafford believe that it is the responsibility of us all, as both individuals and corporations, to make choices that are environmentally and socially sound. You, in turn, are supporting this responsible conduct each time you purchase a Trafford book, or make use of our publishing services. To find out how you are helping, please visit www.trafford.com/responsiblepublishing.html

Our mission is to efficiently provide the world's finest, most comprehensive book publishing service, enabling every author to experience success. To find out how to publish your book, your way, and have it available worldwide, visit us online at www.trafford.com/10510

www.trafford.com

North America & international
toll-free: 1 888 232 4444 (USA & Canada)
phone: 250 383 6864 • fax: 250 383 6804
email: info@trafford.com

The United Kingdom & Europe
phone: +44 (0)1865 722 113 • local rate: 0845 230 9601
facsimile: +44 (0)1865 722 868 • email: info.uk@trafford.com

10 9 8 7 6 5 4 3 2

OUR MOAT

"To the question: 'What shall we do to be saved in this world'?
There is no answer but this: 'Look to your Moat'."
(*George Savile, Marquis of Halifax,* 1633-1695)

This royal throne of kings, this sceptre'd isle,
This earth of majesty, this seat of Mars,
This other Eden, demi-paradise,
This fortress built by Nature for herself
Against infection and the hand of war,
This happy breed of men, this little world,
This precious stone set in the silver sea,
Which serves it in the office of a wall
Or as a moat defensive to a house,
Against the envy of less happier lands,
This blessed plot, this earth, this realm, this England,

....

This land of such dear souls, this dear, dear land.
(*William Shakespeare*, 1564-1616)

I had originally intended to title this collection of essays: *Pull up the Drawbridge. We Should Look to Our Moat*. But the only 'drawbridge' on which people and goods can travel is the Channel Tunnel. Tempting a target as this must be to terrorists it seemed a bit against the odds to suggest that it should not be used despite the massive illegal passage of goods and people who come in. It is years since I used it. But I hope that the security measures essential to prevent this illegal pathway into England are continually being strengthened and that the safety of passengers and freight is safeguarded to the ultimate limits of practicability.

As I assert somewhere, these essays may seem defeatist, and perhaps they are. But the Nation, thanks in large measure to the deceit, disloyalty or feeble activities of all but a few politicians, especially in the last decade, and the flood of incomers of varying quality, some of them very bad indeed, our nation, bled white of many of its best and all its wealth in two great wars, is easy meat to be assimilated into a centralised fascist/soviet-style regional behemoth.

Should we succumb, then that surely will be the end of our history. Should we instead manage to pull in and harbour and revive our national strength and those Christian conventions common to many Faiths, which once led us to the peak of civilised world influence, then there seems to me a chance that we may purge ourselves of the evils which now abound. It follows that if we are left to follow our own laws from a sovereign parliament that we should be able, in our own way, to embrace the many legal quality newcomers as we have done through the ages and utilise their skills to the great benefit of them and our Nation. Two matters and two only have to be borne in mind in this great endeavour facing us. We have already reached a population density which is swamping our existing infrastructure, whilst we have grossly neglected building on the one vital technology that would enable us to harness and use our almost limitless coal-producing energy in a far more acceptably environmental mode.

Let Us Look To Our Moat

Contents

Our Moat	iii
Author's Preface	vii
Introduction	xvii
Chapter I Where are We Going?	1
Chapter II Freedom and Democracy	6
Chapter III Yesterday and Today	17
Chapter IV Today and Tomorrow, Britain or England?	27
Chapter V Two Pillars of a True Democracy	35
Chapter VI The United States of America	40
Chapter VII The British Empire and Commonwealth	46
Chapter VIII Energy Security	48
Chapter IX Britain's Defence Strategy.	51
Chapter X Threats and Countermeasures	55
Chapter XI Sovereignty or Subjection	64
Epilogue	81
Conclusion	84
Acknowledgements	87
Appendix	90

Author's Preface

I am old and not very bold. But my current despair is not wholly accounted for by either. As a Race we have not yet recovered from those critical years when the resolute courage and sacrifices of our people saved the World's evolving civilisation. We threw into the struggle all we and the Commonwealth had. But somewhere, somehow, some of our innovative spirit was lost with most of our wealth; and we have sought since, rather unimaginatively and with inadequate means, to rebuild our international influence and a pattern of society not always relevant to the helter-skelter advances of many aspects of life today.

After winning any struggle, from the boxing ring to a war, Mankind needs a period of recuperation. This was not granted us as wars and threats of war and economic crises multiplied. Our English traditions and our Christian Faith dictated that we should forego any such much needed national rest. And that was our mistake. Now failure to understand what has been happening to society in our Island State since World War II has led us to neglect the more appropriate updating of those foundations of freedom, democracy and our unique form of parliamentary governance on which we have been building for a thousand years, and which have been an exemplar to the world.

The tree of Liberty grew and changed and spread,
But the seed was English.
(The White Cliffs of Dover)

These essays are among the many I have written, some for the Press, some for my friends, in the last ten years as our ship of state shudders to a standstill. Our leaders have not understood that our Anglo-Saxon-Celtic-French stock, whose roots of liberty grow deep, is only reluctantly accepting the massive and wholly uncontrolled immigration by many different (and differing) races and cultures. We are now, with Holland, the third most densely populated nation in the world; and we are only a small island whose boundaries are immovable.

Since the days of Alfred the Great over a thousand years ago, our laws and way of life, lately to a diminishing extent, were among the last remnants of Christianity within an increasingly secular European Christendom born out of the Enlightenment and Descartes *Cogito, ergo, sum*[*]. Now, due to uncontrolled and irreversible immigration a 'New Nation' is growing up with a different culture and with many different creeds and conventions. Like most adolescents we have little idea where we are going; only that, (despite Cicero *Esse oportet ut vivas, non vivere ut edas)*[†] we feel we must enjoy ourselves at all costs.

To exacerbate our difficulties and with no regard to the political deceit involved, we have been hitched to a corrupt European federal behemoth now developing the worst corrupt and dictatorial aspects of both Soviet and Fascist regimes. And to crown our self-inflicted wounds we have suffered for ten years from a two-faced Elective Dictatorship. One face gives us an ostensibly stable econo-

* I think. Therefore I am.

† We ought to eat in order to live, not live in order to eat.

my and the other face a venal sleaze-ridden government which has failed to live up to its promises and has taken us into 'Discretionary Wars' at least five times in ten years. It has burgled our carefully assimilated pension funds, sold off our hard-earned gold reserves just before the anticipated price per ounce escalated and inflicted on us at least 3,000 new laws. And the Queen's Peace no longer prevails over much of the Realm.

My essays will be called defeatist. But I see no hope that we may one day once more contribute that benign influence and unique gift of liberty to an increasingly fractured post-modern world such as we have so greatly contributed in the past. That is, unless we forgo much of our role on the world stage for a few decades (something that will happen anyway if we remain in the European Federation). Such an interregnum as a 'Switzerland' or a 'Norway' will disappoint our leaders used to strutting the world stage as a headline-gripping refuge from domestic pogroms. Such a solution may not work. But it seems to me that only a dramatic change of national posture, perhaps under a 'New Nation Coalition Party' has a chance. If wise leadership is forthcoming such a pause should give us one last chance to meld the old Englishness with the many more recently imported talents. Only thus can we undo the terrible damage to national unity caused by multi-culturism and the allegiance of parliament to the Brussels bureaucracy. It would also give us time to heal the wounds of war which, in parts of the Realm by rotten planning, have left us with mini-communities existing in an even worse state than the Jarrow and other poverty spots those of us alive in the Thirties viewed with such horror. Drugs and booze have today replaced the poverty and Christian forbearance which triggered only a General Strike and the 'Jarrow March' rather than the revolutions that erupted elsewhere.

In this Preface I try briefly to record what was in my muddled wits when reaching these conclusions. I must emphasise, particularly, how the avalanche of rules and regulations, many irrelevant, to which we are now subject by our parliament and the European Union, is breeding not only an army of 'Enforcers' but also an army of 'Informers' (whistle-blowers they are called) resulting in intimidation replacing common sense and sending neighbour against neighbour whilst showing integrity the exit door. It has also helped breed a bigger tribe of 'Yobbos'. Throughout history they have been a small but slowly growing element of our society. They fought (and often won) our wars, they crewed Drake's and Nelson's ships and they formed the bulk of Wellington's victorious armies. Modern western society, as it has evolved in the last two centuries, has little left to offer them. Hitler understood this and created the Gestapo by giving them caps, boots, a uniform and government backing.

"If the whole dead weight of sin were to be allowed to fall upon the law it could not take the strain" proclaimed Lord Justice Devlin. But when law enforcement, faltering under the massive strain by the lack of the Church's moral teaching, occasionally seems likely to achieve its purpose, all too often the criminal leaves the Court a free man or woman. Perhaps Bassanio gives us the answer in *The Merchant of Venice*:

In law, what plea so tainted and corrupt
But being seasoned with a gracious voice.
Obscures the show of evil.

If it has achieved nothing else, this avalanche of laws has surely given us a lawyer's well-paid paradise as he or she persistently evokes the Human Rights Act.

The churches and the legal profession have much to answer for. What about the politicians? A century ago Raymond Asquith wrote of the parliamentary parties: *"The day of the clever cad is at hand. The bleak futility of our public men on both sides is like a flock of sheep playing blind-man's buff in the distance on a foggy day."* Yet those he condemned were as giants compared to many of those we have elected today. And Raymond Asquith was a torch among tapers, as were so many of those legions of leaders from Glenalmond, Ampleforth or Eton, the grammar schools and the other schools or the Liverpool 'Chums' Battalions who gave their lives between 1914 and 1946 that liberty might prevail.

Had it not been for Churchill in 1940, Asquith's *flock of sheep playing blind-man's buff* would have handed us over to a eugenic hegemony in May 1940. As it is, another betrayal had to wait a score of years before we were deceitfully ushered into the European Union.

Finally, there is 'Fear' of which I have written. In a *Daily Telegraph* review of a book *In the Shadow of Death, Living outside the Gates of Mauthausen,* Sir Dirk Bogarde wrote of fear. And since I happened to loiter near Mauthausen while climbing and walking in Austria in the Thirties, I have kept his review. The Austrian people I met were the ordinary gentle folk one finds in rural communities everywhere. But in this case, as we in this country are starting to, they succumbed to fear. This is part of Bogarde's review:

> *Horowitz describes vividly the construction of Mauthausen, the most vicious and hideous and probably the least well known of the camps for the Jew's annihilation, in a quarry three miles from a pleasant little village and a few yards from two thriving farms, set in the gentle rolling hills of southern Austria. Everyone saw it being built, everyone knew it was there, no-one, it seems, dared to ask why. Local people worked for it as carpenters, telephonists, secretaries, typists, plumbers and all the rest.*
>
> *People knew. They heard the sounds, saw the smoke from the furnaces, smelled it as the wind carried it across the woods and fields, leaving greasy deposits of soot on the hay in the meadows and on the washing on the line. No-one raised a finger, no-one questioned even though latterly they watched the shuffling lines*

> *of people being marched through the streets, staring, terrified, lost. Fear ruled. Fear won.*

And in another review on the same subject Bogarde wrote: "*Fear is the predominant feeling. There were many good people in Germany and Austria. People as appalled as we are who have come to know what took place in that decade, but the great majority were ruled by terror for themselves or their children. The Nazis had absolute power and froze any protests or questions, by the severest punishments. People did cry out in horror, they did protest, they did hide their friends and they paid the most terrible price if found out.*"

How, we may well ask could all the good Germans be trapped by fear. I believe it is happening here. My fishmonger has given up his business after a Council-employed *agent provocateur* trapped him into selling fish by the pound; and the same fate could hit our greengrocer with his apples. Another good man from the North died early as a result of his prosecution over his sale of bananas. Our village carnival is slowly being whittled away by health and safety rules. Our bonfire night is under threat. Our brave eighty-year-old churchwarden breaks the law every time he mounts a ladder to renew a light bulb. Already in parts of England Christmas lights are forbidden for fear of offending other Faiths. Fear is taking hold. Mini-Gestapos are being born.

In every society there are pygmies who seek to be recognised by the State and to be given power. And the more rules there are the more of them have to be brought out of the woodwork to wield power. Our uniformed police service has trebled since I was young. But crimes per policeman have mounted a hundredfold. Then there are those with nothing better to do, the Union-Jack underpants fraternity. They follow our foreign-owned, foreign-managed, partially foreign-manned football teams all over the world to wreck bars and Channel ferries and railway carriages and football stadiums. They seem to rampage everywhere. And who dares stop them? Or the muggers? Who dares interfere with a rape or a mugging in the street? We dare not. **You can die that way.** Every day brings its Press-reported stabbing. So too it was in Germany and parts of Austria in the mid-Thirties. Fear won.

A decade ago we had a pension scheme the envy of the world. Thanks to our infamously incompetent chancellor it is in ruins and an old age in poverty beckons. We have become a frightened nation. And there is already a constant search "How do I get round it" as new laws forbid long-cherished practices. Like our Christian heritage our law-abiding society is crumbling. We are the sexual cesspit of Europe and top of the drug addiction league.

Finally I come to the focal point of our problems. With so much destruction of our unique form of governance as our crooked politicians have contrived, how shall we ensure our safety whilst trying to put things right? There is a new nation evolving in Britain. Much has gone wrong as the old verities are forgotten and the foundations of our freedom crumble. There is much still to lose. Terrorism is on the march.

What then should be the strength and configuration of our Armed and Security Forces? The answer of course must depend on resources. The difference between the £15 billion plus we pay annually to a corrupt Europe and the sum (between £250 million-£300 million) that Switzerland or Norway pay, must provide the answer to our safety, as it could contribute to the resources needed to revamp our industry, ensure our own energy supply and create a wealthy 'New Nation' hardworking and at peace with itself.

The answer seems self-evident. We must first renegotiate our relationships with Europe and steer ourselves towards the arrangements in place for Norway and Switzerland.

Should these major negotiations fail then we shall find ourselves as a minor cog in what I have termed this Neo-Soviet/Fascist utterly corrupt European Federation. And our world-admired Armed Forces, such as we seem able still to recruit, but due to inadequate resources and incompetent management, fail properly to equip, will be used as a twenty-five-nation talking shop may ultimately decide.

Should such negotiations succeed even to a more modest conclusion than the Swiss or the Norwegian then several possibilities present themselves to confront the global threat of terrorism and the rising incidence of natural disaster and areas of conflict, whilst at the same time ensuring the security and time to rebuild our fractured nation.

A reconfiguration of our armed and humanitarian task forces on land, in the air and at sea will take decades. The primary aim, within such resources that can be made available, is that they should be able to protect us from the rapidly increasing world threat from rogue states of nuclear attack or war, by the possession and regular up-dating of our 'Indestructible Retaliation', our Trident Submarine Force. But perverted science is providing present and future generations of 'dirty' nuclear and biological weapons besides the conventional terrorists' bombing armoury.

These two major goals, the reconstruction of a nation that is now, reportedly, the third most densely populated nation in the world and the securing of its safety seem to me only to be possible if one condition is accepted.

That condition will be the establishment of a cross-Party 'New Nation' Coalition with a single primary aim: **"To pull up the drawbridge and look to our own moat."** Such a coalition would need to last long enough to create and then devote the maximum resources obtainable to bringing a greater degree of domestic peace and better welfare within this newly-evolving Realm. With the new middle classes in 'Chindia' expanding at an exponential rate, the race is on to meet their demands for goods and services. Britain has a high reputation in both, but the Country must be far more at peace with itself if we are to produce and sell the goods and ideas to time and at a competitive cost. As it is, education and skills are both dropping, whilst the Chancellor's carefully-concealed pension theft has begun to anger the work force.

For the next hundred years, if our industries are to survive, a whole new leadership with better management and research skills needs to be bred, and bred quickly. But managing and leading are different arts. Both are needed. Management can be taught: leadership has to be built onto character which has first to be recognised and cultivated, often a difficult task in a busy school. And if there are leaders, there have to be followers.

- **Leadership is power governed by principle ... directed towards raising people to the highest levels of personal motive and social morality and tested by the achieving of results measured by original purpose.**
- **Power manipulates people as they are: Leadership, as they could be.**
- **Power Impacts: Leadership engages.**
- **Power tends to corrupt: Leadership to create.**

We must aim for a new aristocracy: an aristocracy with brains and character.

Future leaders need both qualities in full. But there is also a need for followers with brains and followers with character. Only by an education system with these simple but difficult targets to implement can we achieve the optimum.

After six years as Chairman of Governors of a school founded nearly a century ago by a very rich man, I became acquainted with a school which has this process as its explicitly defined mission. It quite deliberately sets out to bring both qualities of brains and character, in whatever initial degree they are possessed, simultaneously to the highest limits of individual personalities. When asked to quote an example of what I mean, I quote the case of a boy from a poor background who received an almost free education from

8-17. He won a scholarship to Oxford: he became a first-rate pianist. In his busy life he learnt to climb: in due course he scaled the Matterhorn. But there were many boys and girls like him: potential leaders and managers of the future.

A major reconfiguring of our armed and security and humanitarian forces on the lines later suggested to help confront those terrorist evils now afflicting the world (and soon perhaps a resurgent Russia already showing signs of copying the most malign aspects of the Soviet Union) should occupy only part of the national effort. They are the essential security net to safeguard OUR (new) British way of life founded on OUR Christian heritage of freedom and liberty, and OUR industry and, when within our means, to help friends in trouble. If we are to "Look to our moat" we have to create the wealth and use our taxes more wisely to boost the only means of OUR survival – the inbred brain and muscle power of this 'New Nation' as it strives to live up to the great heritage, our legacy from those who have gone before us and our duty to those as yet unborn.

Introduction

Most of the recent errors of mankind
Have drawn new vigour from a German mind.
Since Humbolt gave a wrench to cultured life,
And started seminars of senseless strife –
Where half a dozen madmen round a table
Turned myth to history, or fact to fable –

... No English studied Marx for good or bad
Nor could have comprehended if they had.
None shared the Marxist principles of hate
That poison prophets of his "better State".

... And all is quagmire where we thought we stood;
And no clear signpost guides us on the way
That leads through life's fogs of varying grey,
So, having made the whole of life unsure,
Hegel retreats to Prussia for his cure ...
(*The Ugciad. A History in Heroic Verse.* Hugh Plommer)

I have lived my life in 'The Age of Communism'. An atheist ideology which asserts, briefly and broadly, that *'Man is just a tool-making animal'* and that human beings, in the mass, can be treated as a herd of cattle, by forceful central direction.

Since I was seventeen there has been another even more hideous ideology, National Socialism or Nazism. Initially this was an offshoot of Italian 'Fascism' (Fasces were bundles of rods with an axe, the symbol of authority of senior magistrates in ancient Rome). Post-World War I Fascism was a dictatorship, but with a largely nominated Assembly, obedient to an unelected Grand Council appointed and presided over by Mussolini.

But National Socialism went much further. It was a dictatorship based on the science of eugenics – the science of breeding. National Socialism's fundamental belief was that by culling the crippled, the unfit, the mentally ill and those of non-Aryan genes and substituting disciplined coupling of the best male and female elements of the population it would be possible to create a Master Race.

Hitler's intention was to carry forward the policy of *Lebensraum*, (Living Space) so ardently pursued in the post-Bismarckian era by the Kaiser. Then, after victory, to spread this grisly eugenics policy throughout first, Western and then Eastern Europe, and then the World. Churchill saw this. Churchill saw also that in world terms it was an ideology more sinister even than Communism because, with what he termed *the help of perverted science*, National Socialism had the potential to reduce Western Civilisation to another Dark Age, from which it might never escape.

It was to overcome this threat to Christian civilisation that Churchill stood like a rock on 27 May 1940, as Holland and Belgium fell, as France tottered, as he seriously anticipated losing the whole British Army on the continent. Those around him, equally agonised, sought to urge him towards 'a more prudent line and to explore possible terms for peace.' He alone saw such a policy as a *slippery slope* down which, if we started, we should never stop. Western civilisation as we knew it, Churchill believed, would disappear perhaps for ever. In fact the final price of salvation from the then German and, later, Japanese policies, conservatively estimated and excluding the China/Japan War pre-1941 war, was 40 million dead; nearly half (18.2 million) being civilians; and one third of those were Jews.

In 1940, if few understood the full significance of what was at stake, it was because of Churchill's vision and rhetoric that so many of my generation, whether from Britain and the Commonwealth and Colonies or the United States, or from those who had escaped the early slaughter and quick disaster to their Countries by the German onslaught, willingly offered or were made to risk their lives.

In the ensuing six years, as Germany surged triumphant through Europe and Africa and over the Oceans, Britain alone lost 326,000 servicemen and 62,000 civilians killed besides some 35,000 of many races drowned in the Merchant Marine.

In a keynote speech to a large audience in Chicago in 1979 (published in my *Old Loves Return*) at a conference on Future Strategic Direction, I quoted the last line of a poem written by Captain Patrick Hore-Ruthven just before he was killed in the Western Desert, '*Man tramples his laws alone.*' And I asked '*Do we not all feel the same developing sense of helplessness stealing numbingly over our minds as the currents of destiny sweep us along*?'

Now, twenty-five years later, despite the ending of the Cold War against the Soviets (as Churchill forecast) I feel this same overwhelming sense of utter impotence. Few people as yet fully comprehend Germany's astonishing material and psychological resurgence from its loss of (probably) 3.5 million servicemen and 2.2 million civilians. Triggered by the Marshall Plan, encouraged by Churchill's '*In Victory, Magnanimity*,' Germany has been transformed by the *alumni* of the Hitler schools, picked young people sent at seventeen to low casualty posts, giving them a better chance of survival to build the future. It is relevant also that the similar schools the National Political Education Academies (NPEAs) which Hitler established in the conquered nations, preached the same 19th and 20th century German policy of European Union. Thus the goal of three wars in 60 years, the first to show France the 'mailed fist', and two deadly world-wide conflicts, is now well on the way to fruition but by more peaceful scheming: namely, the European Union.

Germany has put eugenics on one side. Deliberately of course, because the World will never forget the slaughter of six million Jews and countless Gentiles in the pursuit of a Master Race. Frenchmen, Belgians and particularly Dutch politicians, and again *alumni* from Hitler schools in the once conquered countries and others from the USA and UK, genuinely believe today that to bring Germany into a European family unit is the only way to stifle, perhaps for ever, Germany's ruthlessly effective warrior spirit.

Today Germany no longer needs to pursue the eugenics route. She lit the scientific fuse. Now the Bio-Geneticists of other nations are leading western society down that fearful road. Abortions as a medical need are one thing; abortion as a convenience or for a suspect foetus is another. Fertility Science, brought into adolescence by Hitler's scientists, and grown up by other nations since, **animal and human cloning, designer babies**, such developments are altogether a quite different kettle of fish. All this is well on the way, and until the products in the shapes of adult men and women appear, no-one will know exactly what horrors science has produced.

Historically France, bled white at Verdun and elsewhere, was largely (but in the context of those years) understandably responsible for the now manifest errors in the Versailles Treaty which, in a decade, produced Hitler and then World War II. And in the post-World War II era, with the de Gaulle/Adenauer handshake, Germany recognised that she alone could never dominate Europe. But Adenauer saw that Germany, if coupled to a still-fearful but ostensibly friendly France and the other scared nations, took the initiative, Europe could in time be hers. And so it is happening. Sometimes one, sometimes the other takes the lead. Germany just waits. The German wartime generation that fought and suffered and has rebuilt, has almost disappeared. But the memories of the wartime children remain. They will never permit what they endured to be inflicted on their own offspring. Decades, of a kind of peace from continental war are a probability. The heavy price levied by Germany on the world will gradually be forgotten and one day, perhaps, forgiven, but Germany's desire to be 'top dog' remains. The genes of the Visigoths and the Ostrogoths merging with those of the Huns, still live.

And now I turn to Britain's place in this European imbroglio. Unlike France, Britain's long crusade between 1939-45 had to be paid for with every penny of the wealth that previous generations had garnered. She ended the War with debts that future generations have had to meet; and 400,000 (service and civilian) deaths. On top of this we could never have conquered had not the United States' policy of Lease Lend, paid for by US taxpayers and heavy American casualties, come to our aid. While we fought alone we paid for everything until, our bank balance exhausted, Roosevelt responded to Churchill's plea '*Give us the tools and we will finish the job.*'

But as the war ended Lend Lease stopped. And servicemen returning from years of hardship and battle, found bread rationed as it never was throughout the war, meat virtually non-existent. (It was always a source of post-war cynical comment 'on France's ordeal', that like many others from Britain on duty visits to Paris in the Forties, this writer never returned without several pounds of beef from the plentiful supply bought cheaply in Les Halles).

After World War II the British *classe politique* believed, quite wrongly, that the nations of Europe would be deeply grateful to Britain, for our valiant wartime efforts. Certainly there were small pools of Forces gratitude. But Holland, Belgium, France, had all suffered in varying degrees from our bombing, as had Germany to the greatest extent of all. Many 'high-ups' in Holland never forgave Montgomery for his failure to capture Antwerp, thus condemning them to the 1944 winter diet of tulip bulbs. The Belgians never forgave us for the (unjustified) statements in 1940 that it was the unexpected surrender of the Belgian Forces that triggered Dunkirk. France never forgot Oran or the terrible civilian casualties from the US/UK concentrated pre-invasion bombing. We threw Italy out of her African colonies, laid waste to her countryside and with some contempt denigrated her Forces. Many in Germany still criticise Britain for Dresden and for failing to negotiate in 1940 or listen to Hess later; and then join in a crusade against the Soviets. Others ascribed the arrival of German Forces outside Moscow with the onset of a bitter and defeating winter as due to the fatal six-week delay in launching Barbarossa caused by the British Greek/Crete Campaign. Germany's *classe politique* mostly hate Churchill's memory and, on the whole the German Government since the War has greatly preferred the French to the UK/US occupying forces. The UK/US bombing campaign killed 600,000 German civilians – many books are now being written in Germany condemning this as a moral outrage.

So when the Macmillan Government, looking for a new role as the British Empire crumbled and the Government's European Free Trade Policy, rather patronisingly sought membership of the already well-established European Economic Community, de Gaulle rejected us. He understood British world-wide interests and our relationship with America rather better than Macmillan and, in particular, Heath, whose distaste for all things American and love of Germany is notorious. With de Gaulle dead, Pompidou, seeing a chance to diminish Britain's prestige then still accruing from Britain's courageous wartime role compared to France's 1940 collapse, accepted Britain's request. Pompidou's revealing phrase when negotiating British entry with Heath says it all. '*Je la veux nue*' (I want her [in the EEC] naked).

So we joined the European Economic Community (EEC): and we thought that was all – or the majority of us did. But the price we still have to pay in pounds sterling is exorbitant; our fisheries have gone and the avalanche of petty regulations (so far [2003] 200,000) emanating from the EEC, as it has been translated in the European Community and then the European Union, stifles us.

The Soviet Union has recently imploded and the pace of advance towards a United States of Europe has accelerated. As Britain's naïve (or worse) politicians have led us by the nose away from our democratic past we are, perhaps too late realising that our sovereign parliament is no longer sovereign. Our common law is relentlessly depreciated. *Habeas Corpus* is taking a back seat. A new European Law *Corpus Juris* is being introduced to bind us. 'Whistle-blowing', entrapment, *agents provocateurs* are encouraged. Our highways have a European nomenclature. And finally a reasonably competent ex-ship's steward (turned better-rewarded politician) has divided the Kingdom into eight regions. These are designed to coincide with the eight small regions representing all that will be left of our Nation in a fascistic European behemoth. And to crown it all, over-crowded as we already are in our small island, our welfare state is the attractive haven now sought by an avalanche of emigrants from half the countries of the world.

The American journalist Dorothy Thompson spent much time in Germany in 1940 talking to Nazi theorists about their plans for Europe. In the *Herald Tribune* of 31 May 1940 she wrote:

> *The Germans count upon political power following economic power. Territorial changes do not concern them because there will be no 'France' no 'England' except as language groups. Little immediate concern is felt regarding political organisations … No nation will have control of its own financial or economic systems or its customs.*

As I have said earlier, the German governments today, with the unspeakable crimes of their predecessors engraved forever in the scroll of history, fully understand that no longer can Germany aspire to a unilateral hegemony. An obsequious France must share the load of leadership and Britain as a nation, must not be excluded as de Gaulle wished. Rather Britain must be brought in to be systematically immolated and Anglo-Saxon influence finally abolished from the European concert of nations. Such was the aim of Maastricht and its successor treaties signed by our naïve, ignorant or, arguably, treasonable politicians.

All this was made clear as long ago as 1995 by Rodney Atkinson and Norris McWhirter in their *Treason at Maastricht*. But a dithering Prime Minister, a Conservative Government and Labour Opposition, both with a fair number of obedient nonentities, party hacks or European fellow travellers, and a Lib-Dem group firmly believing in the abandonment of Britain, conspired, by a small (whipped) majority, to pass the Act ratifying the Treaty of Maastricht. Worse has followed at Amsterdam and Nice and since, as British influence is reduced and Britain's interests overruled or discarded.

In 1997, Party corruption and Conservative dithering from a priapic Prime Minister downwards brought in New Labour, full of attractive ideas, pressure groups and ruthlessly skilled 'spin' doctors. Socialist solutions to prevailing problems and other policies irrelevant and often harmful to the general interest of the Nation began to be built on an improving (but inherited) economic base. With the arrival of New Labour the Nation's betrayal into Europe moved quickly to the edge of the slope. In an attempt to advertise Britain's influence and military power, British Forces were injected, arguably illegally, into the Balkans. And standards of probity of the new Administration quickly fell below even those of their predecessors; and have continued a downward trend ever since.

So much for the State. Unhappily the Church of England also continues to pursue its downward path of the last half-century. Pressure groups in the Synod demand further illiterate liturgical change and other actions likely to impede our search for Faith. The Bishops neglect the spiritual duties for which they were consecrated and burble on about political matters that they believe will bring them popularity.

Scientists put it about that they have found the secrets of life. More and more as the Bishops retreat into the oddities and attractions of the material world, more and more as they fail to show us the bridge to eternity, a new secular continental society is developing. It seems to be similar to that which Aldous Huxley envisaged might occur 600 years hence under the atheistic embrace of perverted science. *Cloned alphas* at the top of the human chain, *cloned epsilons* at the bottom. Is this perhaps the future that Germany seeks? It seems little different to that brave new world which they so ruthlessly sought half a century ago.

There are still a few of us alive who watched Italy and then Germany sink into the abyss of dictatorship, while the other governments of Europe, with the exception of brave Poland and Scandinavia, behaved like frightened rabbits.

Stalin wrote in 1942:

> *Divide the world into regional groups as a transitional stage to world government. Populations will more readily abandon their national loyalties to a vague regional loyalty than they will for a world authority. Later the regionals can be brought all the way into a world dictatorship.*

Stalin of course was wrong. As has been visible since the end of the Soviet Union, its various elements, to different degrees, have reverted to their age-old nationalities and customs. Human nature is such that nations with long histories, as most nations in Europe possess, cannot be cast into a melting pot. In the massive emigration into a land still largely unoccupied and with plenty of space, and building on English ideas of democracy, much has been achieved in the USA. But to inject 25 or more European States with histories and customs of their own into a United States of Europe at the speed with which the power-hungry (mostly failed) politicians are seeking to do, is a recipe for war or revolution. While in England's case, further to try to inject the one lonely island, whose laws and customs, almost uniquely in Europe, date back 1,000 years or more, into this vast conglomerate, whose societal *mores*, controls and laws are autocratic, born of revolution and wholly different to England's common law, seems madness.

> *'America is God's crucible, the great Melting Pot where all the races of Europe are melting and re-forming ... here you stand in your fifty groups, with your fifty languages and histories, and your fifty blood-hatred and rivalries ... A fig for your feuds and vendettas! Germans and Frenchmen, Irishmen and Englishmen, Jews and Russians – into the Crucible with you all. God is making the American.'*
> (Israel Zangwin, *The Melting Pot*)

But even in America, populated in quite different and much more favourable circumstances, the Melting Pot has not yet worked out. And it has taken two centuries, a most bloody civil war and many terrible happenings since, to reach the present democratic but still emerging multi-ethnic society where total assimilation is seen to be impossible and not necessarily desirable. But already the Fascist architects of the future Unites States of Europe under a semi-senile President of France are sketching the procedures for choosing not one but TWO Dictator/Presidents of the United States of Europe (USE).

So the Country into which I was born and for which, with millions of others I fought, is now being betrayed into a vast, ungovernable, secular empire. That potential empire's bureaucrats notoriously lack probity and yet are installed above the law. Its governing bodies have fascistic tendencies and lack democratic accountability. Its laws, born of recent bloody revolution, differ fundamentally from those that have evolved in England over the centuries. It's manners, customs, are entirely alien.

In his chapter 'What on Earth was England' from his book *England: an Elegy*, Professor Roger Scruton has described a world which a hybrid like me, a quarter French/Jersiaise Huguenot refugee, a quarter Scots, a quarter Welsh and only a quarter English has enjoyed, as all who cherish freedom can enjoy. It is not difficult to discern what my grandchildren will lose when '*the last years of England*' have passed into the ashes of history, into Prescott's eight regions of his United States of Europe.

So, as I write to the papers, as I contribute to a political party, as I write countless letters, as we seem, as a Nation to slither downhill, I constantly ask myself 'Is it worth bothering?' Should I not just let the world go by? At 91, what does it matter to me?

> *Should I* meekly accept the leadership of the many Church of England Bishops and Priests who, today, no longer seem to believe in the Resurrection and constantly fail to tell us a way over the Bridge to Eternity?
>
> *Should I* accept that due to the Church's incompetence and this lack of leadership the majority of the young have turned their back on Christianity?
>
> *Should I* accept that we are now governed by an elective dictatorship anxious to take our Nation into a 'European Union of the Regions' with ominous Fascist leanings?
>
> *Should I* accept that a large proportion of MPs are morally corrupt and put their own or their Party's interests before loyalty to the Crown and Country?
>
> *Should I* accept that Privy Counsellors who have sworn an oath of loyalty to the Monarch and who have also sworn a similar oath to the European Union, cannot ever be trusted again?
>
> *Should I* accept the increasing regulation of people's lives and the constant blatant manipulation of opinion?
>
> *Should I* accept the sidelining of our age-old 'Common Law' and the infiltration of *Corpus Juris* spewed by the French Revolution?

Should I accept that government ministers increasingly approve oppressive legislation without parliamentary debate?

Should I accept the continuing and steady government inspired demeaning of the Monarchy, our last bastion against the dictatorship New Labour increasingly seems to seek?

Should I accept that our once United Kingdom, thanks to New Labour, is now far from united?

As one of those fortunate to live through World War II *should I* renounce those words at the Royal Naval College at Dartmouth on the Memorial to my many friends who gave their lives that the Nation might live?

> "See that ye hold fast the heritage we leave you, YEA AND TEACH YOUR CHILDREN ITS VALUE, that never in the coming centuries their hearts may fail them or their hands grow weak".

Is there anything left worth fighting for? Where in fact do I stand? What is my heritage?

It was Justice William O Douglas of the United States who wrote:

> "As nightfall does not come at once, neither does oppression. In both instances there is a twilight when everything, seemingly, remains unchanged. And it is in such twilight that we all must be aware of change in the air – however slight – Lest we become unwilling victims of the darkness."

Change indeed is in the air and I have been forced to believe that our 1,000-year-old continually evolving English parliamentary democracy, indeed Western Christian civilisation itself is heading for a long dark tunnel. It was Lord Justice Devlin in his notable Maccabaean Lecture who warned us in 1958 that *'If the whole dead weight of sin were ever to be allowed to fall upon the law it could not take the strain … Without the help of Christian teaching the law will fail'*. Christian teaching is now minimal. Crime soars.

Old age creates conservatism with a small c. But experience transcends book learning and theory. I see 'nightfall' ahead. As a Nation unwillingly tied to Europe, and with a creeping Islam, it seems indubitable, we shall soon enter a similar Dark Age to that Christendom endured as the Roman Empire faded. So with the constant encouragement of a loving and devoted wife I try to sound the alarm to my grandchildren

> *Violent crime is escalating as never before.*
>
> *Personal integrity and honesty are becoming increasingly rare.*
>
> *Drugs and TV pervert and subvert the bodies and souls of our citizens, particularly the young.*
>
> *The Monarchy and Parliament and our Common Law, respectively the centuries-old pillars of our Nation's stability and unwritten Constitution, are individually derided, bypassed or undone by a 1997 leadership with Cromwellian instincts.*
>
> *Not since Cromwell has our Parliament passed into such a fearful and impotent apathy as it displays today. As Italian democracy yielded to Mussolini, Weimar to Hitler, so Britain, girding its executive in fascist clothes is yielding to a fully Fascist European Union of the Regions.*

WE MUST LOOK TO OUR MOAT

The threat comes in a multiplicity of forms. Secularisation and progressive authoritarianism is a subtle process that seems to be proceeding with no end in sight. None of us is immune.

I look back to a night just sixty years ago. Our ship had been torpedoed and all of us from the Admiral to the youngest Boy Seaman, probably aged about 17, were in the choppy sea, as our home for less than two years of active death-dealing warfare, reared up and slipped back stern first to the seabed six hundred feet below.

At first there were signs of distress and cries for help. Leading Stoker Davies, one of several in a fine ship's company who had been wounded and sent to hospital but had fought his way back to us, was a Welshman with a lovely voice. Quite suddenly as HMS *Naiad* slipped away and as we gave her a farewell cheer, he broke into 'Abide with me …' Most of us knew part of it. Davies knew it all. And as he sang the last verse, of which the last line seemed particularly appropriate:

'Hold Thou Thy Cross before my closing eyes;
Shine through the gloom, and point me to the skies:
Heaven's morning breaks, and earth's vain shadows flee;
In life, in death, O Lord, abide with me.'

a quite astonishing peace descended on us all. Was it perhaps *'The peace of God which passeth all understanding'*? And when later the destroyer did arrive out of the dark the scene changed. Life suddenly seemed very important as we swam towards her, helping those burnt or wounded. Davies, a strong swimmer helped many to the jumping nets where the experienced crew of HMS *Jervis* pulled them up. As Davies finally reached the deck his brave heart gave out; and he died.

Sir George Mallaby under whom I worked between 1948-50, when he was Secretary General of the Brussels Treaty Organisation from which NATO evolved, suggests in his *Studies of Men in Power* that in the post-retirement phase of a man's life *"There are the correspondence columns of* The Times *to keep filled, schools with their tribal proceedings of speech day to be attended and other occupations which appear to welcome the ruminations of old age."* When that phase is over Sir George recommends that, *"As the tried and faithful husband of his loving wife everyone should, like Plantin 400 years ago, peacefully await in his own home the welcome arrival of Death."*

Whether from arrogance, impatience or because of my loving wife's staunch Christian Faith and enthusiasm for a better world that drives me on, the last part of Sir George's prescription has not seemed possible to follow. A European monster of fascistic tendencies awaits us with unprecedented powers to do our Country ill.

I believe everything that our Nation has stood for and all that we of the older generation fought for is being squandered by British politicians, many of whose habits and calibre remind me precisely of Kipling's *Bandar-log.*

Milton! thou shouldst be living at this hour:
England hath need of thee: she is a fen
Of stagnant waters: altar, sword and pen,
Fireside, the heroic wealth of hall and bower,
Have forfeited their ancient English dower
Of inward happiness.

(Wordsworth)

AGAIN I SAY: "WE MUST LOOK TO OUR MOAT"

1

Where are We Going?

Where are you going?
We don't know.
What are you doing?
We can't say.
(*Paint Your Wagon*, 1948)

A birth rate of 2.1 births per woman is needed to stabilise a population. In today's Old Engla-Lond, the sum of the invasions of an island of Celts by Romans, Angles, Saxons, Jutes, Danes, Normans and other European tribes, the figure has dropped to 1.8. In this, the white non-Muslim population of England, the average age is 41: in the Muslim element, it is 28: while the Muslim birth rate/woman exceeds 2.1

The birth rate in the rest of Europe is, in most cases, even lower than in England: Germany 1.4, Greece 1.3, Italy 1.2, Spain 1.1 and Russia 1.0 (figures from the Internet).

The signpost says: *To the browning and Brown-ing of Britain.* And Europe, the foundation of Christendom, is going the same way.

Here, in the once United (now only partially united) Kingdom we are, quite literally, seeing the birth of a New Nation, no longer 'Engla-Lond' but a small part of what may soon be called Eurabia. The teaching of the Qu'ran in our *Madrassas* is beginning to overtake the teaching of the Bible in church (allegedly Christian) schools. These and other reasons, are leading to a steady trickle of some of our best people to various nations of the Commonwealth and the USA.

Many of the best genes that contributed to the greatest Empire the World has known lie buried in the ocean deep, the sands of Africa and in other foreign fields. France, that great nation, collapsed in 1940 from a lack of firm leadership due to the blood-letting of World War I. It was in the same war and World War II when alone, but for the Commonwealth and little Poland, Britain 'held the fort' against a vile ideology, that many of our Nation's best blood lines were lost. It was some of these, over the previous 2,000 years who helped to put the 'Great' into Britain. Now they are gone forever. And with them inspirational leaders like Pitt, Lloyd George or Churchill.

Because of this sacrifice, apart from one short period in the 1980s, when a great prime minister was betrayed by craven underlings, no leaders have emerged to steer us into calmer waters. So the population density of this small island is exceeded in the whole world only by Bangladesh and South Korea. We are full to the brim. And there is nothing we can do about it. Yet under an incompetent administration the inflow continues or even accelerates. And a New Nation has been born facing ten major threats, several of them potentially mortal.

Here they are!

TEN NATIONAL THREATS

1. Near anarchy, as a direct consequence of multi-culturism and the ethnic ghettos now firmly established in so many towns. Here is a torch ready to be lit.

2. Foreign criminal mafias spreading drugs and prostitution. Home-grown and foreign terrorists armed with nuclear, bio and chemical weapons.

Both 1 and 2 are the result of incompetent immigration control in the last decade and membership of the free frontier European Union

3. For the first time in 150 years, Britain will soon be dependent on foreign energy sources. This is due to lack of governmental foresight and the destruction of the coal mines, as well as governmental preoccupations with armed conflict of doubtful legality, of no relevance to national interests and undertaken mainly to divert public attention from the failure of domestic policies.

4. The Sovietisation of health and education and other services by centralisation and nationalisation. Employees have been guaranteed early pensions.

5. Gradual destruction of the loyalty and devotion and so recruitment and retention of the Armed Forces of the Crown. This is due to a lack of battlefield resources needlessly sold off, the continual use of our armed forces as mercenaries in conflicts of little threat-relevance to the Nation (and of doubtful legality) and the needless prosecution of soldiers for alleged heat-of-battle or post-heat-of-battle misconduct.

6. A parliament, still sovereign, but with an elected administration constantly and carelessly subordinating that sovereignty to permit legislation by a corrupt European Union to become Law of the Land, often contravening England's long-held freedoms.

7. The virtual abandonment of Cabinet Government in favour of the worst type of presidential rule. The Queen's First Minister appears to consult mainly with a small unelected self-opinionated clique.

1. Following 7 (above), the deliberate sidelining of the monarchy at every opportunity. Privy Council lifelong oaths of loyalty to the Crown and subsequent oaths of loyalty by ex-ministers to the European Union, conflict.

2. Secularisation and the abandonment of Christianity as the national religion.

3. As a direct result of all the above, there is a widespread but still passive dismay. This is turning to a search for means of more active dissent. The Nation is no longer at peace with itself.

To sum up: *We have lost our way. We are becoming a New Nation and we must find a peaceful way forward.*

What is it that most of us in this Country, whatever our colour, religion or origin would wish to see defended? Amongst many aspects of modern life, probably at least the following:

- The Monarchy
- Our sovereign parliament exercising its authority within our unwritten Constitution
- The spirit of Magna Carta
- Habeas Corpus

- Our Common Law
- Trial by Jury for most criminal cases
- Freedom of religion
- Freedom of the Press
- Politically independent civil and defence services
- National energy sufficiency to support an increasing standard of living
- A thriving export trade

But beyond the above, the majority look for good education opportunities for all. For an aristocracy of brains and character. For peaceful streets, freedom from terrorism and a non-political police service. An efficiently managed health service available to all, fairly funded as a percentage of income. Above all, we look for a new culture deriving from the great traditions of our past and the best of the evolving wonders of benign science and engineering.

2

Freedom and Democracy

Who could have dreamt
That times should come like these!
Remnant of Honour, tongue tied with contempt,
Consider: you are strong yet, if you please.
A hundred just men up, and arm'd but with a frown,
May hoot a hundred thousand false loons down,
Or drive them anyway like geese.
But to sit silent now is to suborn
The common villainy you scorn.

(*Coventry Padmore*)

FREEDOM

For any attempt to define *Freedom* we should go back to the Great Charter of 1215. Bishops and nobles claimed and secured at Runnymede the rights not of baron and churchman only, but those of freeholder and merchant, of townsman and villein (farmer). Importantly the provisions against wrong and extortion which the barons drew up as *against* the King (today the government) for themselves, they drew up *against* themselves for their tenants. In this way the Great Charter marks the transition from the age of traditional rights, preserved in the Nation's memory, to the age of written legislation, of Parliament and Statutes, which, until recently, we have all enjoyed.

No free man shall be taken or imprisoned or disseised, or outlawed, or exiled, or anyways destroyed; nor will we go upon him, nor will we send upon him, unless by the lawful judgement of his peers, or by the law of the land. To none will we sell, to none will we deny or delay, right or justice.

In his great speech *The Vindication of the Constitution* Disraeli said: '*They were great men, that Archbishop of Canterbury and that Earl of Pembroke who, in the darkness of the feudal ages, laid this bold and broad foundation of our national liberties ... they did not act upon abstract principles ... which the first schoolman hired by the king might have refuted; they acted upon positive conventional right ... they established the liberties of Englishmen as a life estate which their descendants might enjoy, but could not abuse or forfeit by any false or fraudulent conveyance. They entailed our freedom.*'

DEMOCRACY

But freedom was not enough. Somehow democracy, the legacy of a city state of free men had to be adapted to the England of Henry III and Prince Edward. Simon de Montfort, that patriot Earl created a popular chamber of two knights from every county, two citizens from every city and two burgesses from every borough. Thus, in 1265, was formed a newly developed Estate of the Realm which today we call the Commons' House of Parliament. And so, telescoping the centuries, with the King's Council, the Earls and Barons and Archbishops and Bishops, (today The House of

Lords) we arrived at the three elements of our constitution which, with but one hiccough, has served the Nation well for close on 700 years. And that one hiccough, lasting as it did through its several stages for just short of fifty years was, in the end, recovered by the instincts of very ordinary Englishmen who managed to destroy a Dictatorship, to bridge the religious chasm dividing the Nation and to set the Crown and Parliament on the path we tread today. And this could, still, just be called 'Democracy'.

The freedoms we enjoy are the cogs and driving wheels of democracy. With a 'New Labour Party' largely conjured up in the years of Opposition by a brilliant lawyer (then Lord Chancellor) and his pupil Mr Blair, one is drawn back to the similarities between General Ireton (the brains) and Cromwell, (the man of action). Today they seem to be intent on building, not a 'New Model Army', but a 'New Model Constitution'. An easy task with a massive parliamentary majority of predominantly young men and women, many with little knowledge of the history of the Mother of Parliaments, of our consequent influence in the real world, and lacking the wisdom that comes only from experience. In effect Britain has now achieved Lord Hailsham's prophecy of an *ELECTIVE DICTATORSHIP*. Oliver Cromwell, crafty and ruthless as occasion claimed, was always a reluctant and apologetic dictator, '*Come, come,*' he concluded his speech to Members, '*I will put an end to your prating. You are no parliament.*' Mr Blair addressed his newly-elected parliamentary colleagues, on 7 May 1997, after an hour of questions and comment, some of it critical: '*Listen. It's not your job to tell us what to do.*'

The Millbank File. A top-level mole told the *Sunday Times*: '*It is a Big Brother File basically. At the end of five years we should have detailed files on everybody. Very few of the new MPs have stepped out of line so far. But if there's a hint of trouble the unit is there to stamp on them.*'

So this Elective Dictatorship, supported by all modern techniques of propaganda and control, such as past dictators would have envied, seems set on, first guillotining through fundamental constitutional changes and then instituting new voting procedures wholly inimical to British traditions of freedom and democracy. So much, we are told, was agreed between the Prime Minister and Paddy Ashdown at what is known in the New Labour and Liberal-Democrat Parties as the *Treaty of Novosibirsk.* (That unlikely venue for the conclusion of an agreement resulted from the aged VC10 carrying the two Leaders from Hong-Kong landing for repairs in Siberia). But that is not the end of New Labour's drive. No doubt with the willing acquiescence of the Liberal-Democrats, having destroyed the *United* Kingdom, this dictatorship intends to harness our Nation's once constituent parts to a Federal Union, via a common currency, under German hegemony, as Albert Speer so planned …

Apart from its two main aims the New Model Labour Party is so arranging the Treasury purse that there will be scope for a substantial 'hand-out' shortly before the next Election. Then total subordination to a European Union and the end of 700 years of increasingly democratic parliamentary government on our Island will be accomplished. (Written in the year 2000).

THE CHURCHES

First and foremost the Anglican Church, or more precisely its prelates, unlike many 'faith full' rectors and vicars seem to have abrogated their responsibilities (and too often it seems, their Faith), in favour of endless 'Synodical discussions', which make headlines from Church House and Lambeth, and severely curtail the time available for the pastoral duties of parish priests. As the Catholic Medical Quarterly has charged, '*the medical profession has assumed an importance once accorded to the priesthood … The new morality is a medical morality, a system of rules for saving the body, rather than the soul …*' or, as the Dean of Peterhouse put it, '*Both in daily life and in the worship of the Church, the prevailing emphasis upon the transformation of the material world has robbed men of their bridge to Eternity …*' Most of our prelates of the Anglican Church seem wholly incapable of distinguishing social deprivation from spiritual impoverishment. '*Faith*', I was taught, and as I have frequently written, '*is reason standing on tiptoe.*' Gone are the Ramsays, the Bardsleys, the Reindorps, the Flemings who, so often, lit the flames of Faith or, at least, provided a ladder to peer over the surrounding walls of disbelief. It took a Solzhenitsyn – speaking moreover in London – to ask '*What happens to a society when men have forgotten God.*' He had noticed the Nation's unawareness of spiritual values, and its empty pews.

SCIENCE

Secondly we are entering a world of perverted science. This is being written at Christmas time. Two thousand years ago, on the first Christmas Day, the population of the planet was about 250 million. Today it is perhaps six billion, increasing at the rate of 200 per minute. Death control has overtaken and superseded birth control. As Aldous Huxley wrote in his *Brave New World Revisited*: '*This fantastically rapid redoubling of our numbers will be taking place on a planet whose most desirable and productive areas are already densely populated, whose soils are being eroded by the frantic efforts of bad farmers to raise more food and whose easily available mineral capital is being squandered with the reckless extravagance of a drunken sailor getting rid of his accumulated pay.*' The Charter of the Institution of Civil Engineers (in part) reads: '… *to direct the great services of power in nature for the use and convenience of man.*' That is a policy now almost entirely ignored by enthusiastic scientists seeking knowledge only for the sake of knowledge or for the sake of power and self aggrandisement, and politicians largely ignorant or neglectful of the paths down which perverted science is taking us. So while 'Death control' outnumbers 'Birth control', genetic manipulation and post-natal conditioning are now facts of life. The latter, now being applied to infants via TV and radio, and certainly to children, adolescents and adults. Cloning and multiple births of high and lower intellectual calibre humans are soon to emerge from Dr Seed's clinic in Chicago. The type of democracy, once suitable for a City State, struggling today to adapt, constantly disappears under the media drive of a multiplicity of single-cause activists, using all the modern facilities of the Internet and the post-modern world to thrust forward their particular, and often selfish, interest.

TELEVISION and RADIO

The problem with both TV and radio is that as they become ubiquitous, as Stations and satellites multiply, the market for entertainers, commentators, teachers, culture, pornographic pimps, constantly expands. And sadly, in the nature of things, the quality of the first four groups diminishes. There are just not enough people of quality in each group to go round. Sadly, too, the type of humour constantly hurtles downhill, mitigated only by the increasingly appalling articulation of the, so-called, funny people. Except for the *News* and a few other programmes with good actors, few can really understand the current gabble.

THE FOUR WORLD STAGES

1) The PRE-MODERN. Feudal and agrarian with a weak but authoritarian military control, with little intellectual basis outside religion or magic scholasticism and chaotic foreign relations usually intent on seeking territory.

2) The EARLY-MODERN. More centralised and organised. Military and diplomatic functions remaining central, but more commercially oriented as the commercial economy begins to dilute the agrarian. The Early-Modern era coincides with a largely rationalist background; while commercial pressures are often a *casus belli*.

3) The LATE-MODERN. Where we are now. Centralised and bureaucratic government, whether ideological, authoritarian or democratic, taking control of education, health, welfare, industry, and military. Economically an era of industrial mass production; Darwinian ideas of progress. Christianity apparently in decline. An era of mass armies and total war.

4) The POST-MODERN. The era into which we may now be entering. In this state power will be much diffused domestically and internationally; but will be always much influenced by media and popular emotion. Pressures by competing activists complicate decision making. Industrial activity gives way to increasingly dominating service and information industries. Christianity apparently still losing ground. Existentialism, Wittgenstein, Einstein, Warhol, etc. Islam advances. Transparency and mutual vulnerability and non-State activists such as Media, Greenpeace, reduction in arms exports, environment *et al*, all play an important part in foreign relations. The time frame for drawing up and enunciating policy shortens.

And to this could now be added increasing terrorism of all kinds.

DEFINITIONS OF DEMOCRACY

'Democracy' is now the word most commonly used in the Press and TV, albeit in the widest variety of contexts. It is plain that the Tories see in it a different meaning to the Lib-Dems and the Lib-Dems to New Labour and New Labour to Old Labour.

Almost every Nation in the UN, even under military or dictator regimes, proclaims that it has, or soon will have, a 'Democratic Government.'

'Democracy,' Admiral Jellicoe once defined as, *'a disinclination to accept any form of restraint, and a desire for unrestricted freedom of life and action.'* A correspondent to the *Nineteenth Century* periodical in

1885 went even further, *'The democratic doctrine is, in its essence, an unconscious expression of envy of anything superior to self, and a vague aspiration that there should be no contrasts between one man's lot and another's …'*

Bernard Shaw said *that 'Democracy substitutes election by the incompetent many for appointment by the corrupt few'.*

Theodore Parker in his great anti-slavery speech 150 years ago defined democracy as *'A government of all the people, by all the people, for all the people; of course, a government after the principles of eternal justice, the unchanging law of God; for shortness sake, I will call it the idea of freedom'.*

So on the eve of its translation from a Dominion to a Sovereign State a British Secretary of State walked to his plane at Lagos through an avenue of ecstatic Nigerians chanting 'Free-Domm, Free-Domm'. (His 'aside' to the High Commissioner is *unprintable*). But it implied that there would probably be less Freedom under 'Self rule' than there had been under Colonial rule. Sadly this has turned out to be true.

Two delightful fellow students of mine at the Imperial Defence College, one, later, the President of Nigeria, were both assassinated.

Hilaire Belloc wrote: *"The accursed power which stands on privilege*
(And goes with Women, Champagne and Bridge)
Broke – and Democracy resumed her reign,
(Which goes with Women, Bridge and Champagne).

Lord Macaulay (perhaps true only until the recent abolition of hereditary Peers): 'Our democracy was, from an early period, the most aristocratic, and our aristocracy the most democratic in the world'.

Schumpeter seemed to believe 'that some form of democracy existed provided "people can choose between elites that will govern them and can renew or expel them at reasonable intervals".

The dangerous sophistry first suggested by Thrasymachus in Plato's *Republic* 'Might is Right' has reappeared through the ages whenever an embryo Dictatorship starts to grow like a cancer in a Nation's womb, as I fear is now starting to grow in our (so far) *'Elective Dictatorship'* under which we now struggle.

In today's world the pen and TV is becoming mightier than the traditional sword usually associated with Dictators. Carefully selected 'Spin' and short 'Sound Bites' are now most effective weapons, providing the only comprehensible language for the majority of a Third Millennium brainwashed Electorate.

> *The foundation of all democracy is that the people have the right to vote. To deprive them of that right is to make a mockery of all the high-sounding phrases which are so often used. At the bottom of all the tributes paid to democracy is the little man, walking into the little booth, with a little pencil, making a little cross on a little bit of paper – no amount of rhetoric or voluminous discussion can possibly diminish the overwhelming importance of that point.*
>
> (Winston Churchill.
> Speech in House of Commons October 31st 1944)

> *Democracy is not self executing. We have to make it work, and to make it work we have to understand it. Sober thought and fearless criticism are impossible without critical thinkers and thinking critics. Such persons must be given the opportunity to come together, to see new facts in the light of old principles and evaluate old principles in the light of new facts by deliberation, debate and dialogue. This, as we all know well, though some of us forget from time to time, requires intellectual independence, impenitent speculation, and freedom from political pressure. For democracy's need for wisdom will remain as perennial as its need for liberty. Not only external vigilance but unending self-examination must be the perennial price of liberty, because the work of self government never ceases.*
>
> (Adlai Stevenson, 1963)

I have the strong view that voting should be compulsory as it is in Australia and in Holland and that there should be a small fine for people who do not choose to execute their civic duty.

(Winston Churchill.
House of Commons. June 23rd 1948)

At a time of turmoil, strife and bloodletting, one can find hope in an expanding democracy rooted in responsibility, actively safeguarded by law.

(A N Spinel, 1969)

The New York Times, 1st June 1940

It was perhaps that great American newspaper which correctly defined what constituted Democracy in Britain in 1940:

THE COMMON MAN

So long as the English tongue survives, the word Dunkirk will be spoken with reverence. For in that harbour, in such a hell as never blazed on earth before, at the end of a lost battle, the rags and blemishes that have hidden the soul of democracy fell away. There, beaten but unconquered, in shining splendour, she faced the enemy.

They sent away the wounded first. Men died so that others could escape. It was not so simple a thing as courage, which the Nazis had in plenty. It was not so simple a thing as discipline, which can be hammered into men by a drill sergeant. It was not the result of careful planning, for there could have been little. It was the common man of the free countries, rising in all his glory out of mill, office, factory, farm and ship, applying to war the lessons learned when he went down the shaft to bring out trapped comrades, when he hurled the lifeboat through the surf, when he endured poverty and hard work for his children's sake.

The shining things in the souls of free men Hitler cannot command, or attain, or conquer. He has crushed it, where he could from German hearts.

It is the great tradition of democracy. It is the future. It is victory.

An afterthought remembering 9/11

Perhaps it would not be too much to place the citizens of New York, the New York Fire Department and the New York Police and those many brave people in the Twin Towers in the same category. Their performance, too, was Democracy at its best.

3

Yesterday and Today

The days when 27,000 allied tanks confronted 52,000 Soviet tanks have gone. Apart from a modified strategic nuclear policy of 'Mutually Assured Destruction' aimed at Rogue States, there is now a change from 'Industry-based War' to 'War amongst People' – terrorism (based on religions and envy) with primitive (but very dangerous) nuclear, biological or chemical weapons and the (probably remote) possibility of more sophisticated conflicts over non-indigenous energy supplies – whilst pictures of humanitarian disasters brought by the Media into comfortable sitting rooms together add to the obvious military need for some sort of reconfiguration of our Armed Forces. But there are other domestic problems demanding action at the same time.

Parliament

The gradual building of the institutions of government that have served the country well for a thousand years of evolving democracy are being destroyed by an administration which, like Hitler, achieved power by strictly democratic means from an impotent Conservative (Weimar-type) lookalike. Just as the Reichstag, after a few months, parliament has become a collection of 'yes' people, working shorter hours. An administration with members who mostly do what the Whips or the prime minister or his deputy (or the EU) tell them to do (except when invited to dismiss Old Labour *shibboleths* particularly in the field of education), and an Opposition, until lately, so wet, so unimaginative, so lazy that it rarely seemed to represent those who voted Conservative.

As this is being written, the government announces the Legislative and Regulatory Reform Bill which, unless abandoned or voted down, will provide this and future administrations with the same opportunity as that which gave Hitler the opening to become Chancellor and destroy all vestiges of democracy. And one has to ask whether the deputy prime minister's sudden enthusiasm for 'cadets' and croquet is because he has just heard of the *Hitler Youth*, the nursery of Nazism which many of us, aware of the poverty of Jarrow and of British youths lounging on street corners with no work for them, so naively admired as the 1930 way forward.

Equally disturbing is the fact that political direction seems not to be set by a Cabinet but by an unelected and what, to many, appears to be a thoroughly untrustworthy entourage in Downing Street or by posses of wealthy New Labour-supporting 'Peership'-seeking nonentities, now allegedly bribing Downing Street or ministers with gifts or loans to the Labour Party Treasury.

Churchill was wrongly blamed for the failure of the Conservative party to win the 1945 election. The Army Education Service had seen to it that the great majority of soldiers believed that the war was a result of Conservative impotence in the Thirties and this belief was widely shared in the Country. It was "time to turn over a new leaf". Churchill may have gone a bit far by equating socialism to the Gestapo in the same sentence. But his broadcast on June 4 1945 seems relevant today: *"Socialism is inseparably interwoven with totalitarianism and the abject worship of the State. Look how even today they hunger for controls of every kind as if they were delectable foods instead of wartime inflictions ... The State is to be the arch-employer, the arch-planner, the arch-administrator and ruler and, the arch-caucus-boss".*

Britain Today

A recent Civitas report recorded that Britain was now *"A seriously crime-afflicted and disintegrating society"*. And it concluded: *"England, from being a society remarkably free of crime and disorder, especially from the middle of the 19th to the middle of the 20th century, by the late 1990s had a worse record than either France, Germany or the United States"*. Where there had been two crimes per police officer (and only 57,000 police officers) in 1921, there were now forty-four crimes per officer with a police force of 134,000 (and several thousand civilian assistants) in 2003/4.

The Prime Minister has admitted, after seven years in office, that even after lowering target standards, one in four children leave primary school without being able to read or count properly. The National Audit Office (2006) reported that *most* school leavers lacked basic literacy and numeracy skills, that twenty-six million adults of working age were in the same position and that the UK has a higher proportion of adults with low levels of literacy and numeracy than thirteen other developed countries. A judge, complaining at an illiterate notice in the Law Courts was told by a more senior colleague that it was the message not the wording that mattered. So far have we sunk.

Any deep examination of the reasons for our plight are beyond the scope of this Essay. Nevertheless, certain ephemeral ideas float around and merit mention. The very scale of immigration (one million) largely Islamic who have been granted British citizenship in the last nine years, while the Human Rights Act has to answer for much of what is going wrong. Rights have become a secular religion and, indeed, have replaced Faith. People feel ill done by. "We ourselves can never be at fault". Expensive litigation followed by compensation from the public purse (filled by taxpayers) is the panacea most now seem to seek whenever misfortune strikes.

Then there is the Welfare State and the reduction of poverty, both noble aims, but aims which create a mind set "That the state must look after me". Altogether, an expensive idea and one to which it is easy to succumb, albeit at limitless cost (£Billions of wrongly distributed Benefits) thanks to Treasury incompetence and Ministerial irresponsibility.

Public debt is said to have reached £1 trillion. With the possibly temporary appreciation of house prices and the ease by which almost blame-free bankruptcy may now be achieved at the expense of someone else's loss, economists call this (just) a 'social problem'. And this it certainly is. To spend without the money to meet the cost is, to most people, gross dishonesty, whether or not it is nationally economically damaging. It is a disease sweeping the country.

Further unrestricted immigration due to government incompetence has permitted entry of foreign mafias, terrorists and criminal gangs, all difficult to police. This has diluted the welcome owed to the necessarily rationed input from abroad of skilled, hard-working and honest citizens. An input which should have been restricted, but was not, to what this small island can accommodate in terms of such simple facts as potable water supplies.

The arrival of many immigrants with different faiths has upset Christian Shepherds used to enjoying capricious synodical whimsies and internal and denominational squabbles. The numbers worshipping at mosques leaves Christians and Jews gasping: and Buddhism has even come to Cornwall.

The Three Theistic Religions

Only 300 years ago, Vienna was under siege by Islam. As this is being written, the latest poll suggests that 40% of Muslims in the UK wish for the introduction of shariah law. But some sanity remains. The (ex-Guyanan) Race Equality Watchdog, Sir Trevor Phillips, is quoted as advising those Muslims who so think, to leave Britain! Whilst an Archbishop of York born of African parents in Uganda, calls for a proper celebration of St George's Day.

Multiculturalism, originally promoted as the answer to the influx of immigrants (and which is still being promoted by the London Mayor with large subventions of taxpayers' money) is proving a disaster. In half a dozen cities English, if it is spoken at all, is very much a second language. Anyone wishing to read the objectively told story of how we have lumbered ourselves with the best of intentions, should read Mr George Alagiah's *A Home From Home* (Little Brown).

Christian and Jewish leaders are becoming aware that they have largely lost their influence amongst the young. They are currently failing to provide youth with a modern and acceptable answer to the question posed in the eighth psalm:

What is man that thou art mindful of him

What is Man? In medico-ethical debates, such as on stem-cell research, pre-natal genetic screening, abortion, the question calls for a definition to clarify the status of the embryo. From which moment on might we speak of a human being? Or which properties do we need to assume before we ascribe to it human dignity? Designer babies are becoming the fashion.

A million foetuses have been aborted in the UK in the last thirty years, most for social, not medical, reasons. Embryos are stacked in refrigerators awaiting a variety of fates. Today's answers to the medico-ethical debate as to 'what Man is' are not easy to discern. Few Divines of any faith attempt to enlighten us, whilst the synod wastes time and money remorselessly pursuing irrelevancies.

Marriage in Britain is no longer regarded as the essential building block of a civilised society. It has given way to what the Government cynically terms 'alternative family forms'. Parenting during the difficult fifty years of possibly imminent extinction by nuclear war provoked a subliminal attitude of: *"Eat, drink and be merry, for tomorrow we die"*. Thanks largely to the United States, we didn't die. Unfortunately, the first two have become a habit and the increasing use of drugs has added to merriness and gross immorality.

The added financial inducements not to marry, and ill-judged articles in the Press emphasising the financial losses incurred if childbearing is preferred to making money, have moved wives and partners towards earning rather than mothering. So childcare, for those who have chanced breeding, has been taken over by expensive primary *kibbutzim* and parental love, which goes with early discipline, is replaced by expensive presents, even in quite poor households. Out-of-wedlock births will soon overtake those from the sacrament of marriage but, demographically, the white, allegedly Christian, population of Western Europe, will soon be overtaken by Asian and Caribbean genes and by Islam. Rudi Dutschke's *Long March of Subversion through the Institutions*, started many years ago, is bearing fruit. The bishops either remain mute or are mutually contradictory. An inexplicable lack of vocation has denuded our Land of priests and, more importantly, of intellectually-endowed truly Christian priests.

Many people, across several generations, now think more of what they can get out of life rather than what they can put in. Binge drinking, drugs and a helter-skelter after casual sex in any form or perversion, despite the frightening increase in sexual diseases, are subliminally and overtly encouraged by the tabloid press, the interminable osculation on television and, even by official sex education booklets.

Family Life

The family is the universal school of life. It is not the preserve of Jew or Christian or Islam. It is the heritage of all humanity. In whatever form or language or rituals in which the great religions engage, there is now no longer much room for God in family life so, in our once United Kingdom, we are becoming a disintegrating society. The basic defence of our national culture has become flawed. These ills of modern British society have their origins in a loss of piety. Our (Christian) church leaders and most of their priests are failing us. Many parochial church councils are just a bad joke. As Edward Norman has written of the Church of England priesthood: *"Their prevailing emphasis upon the transformation of the material world has robbed us of the bridge to eternity. No longer do they speak to us of the evidences of the unseen world amidst the rubble of the present one".*

Fear

The thing I am most afraid of is fear. (Montaigne)

Today we are battered by a tsunami of fear. Children are instructed never to acknowledge a greeting from an adult so they no longer respond to a cheery good morning for fear of sexual attack. Fear of road deaths; railway accidents; burglars; the IRA; terrorists; nuclear war or contamination by a harmless submarine in dock; muggers; MRSA; Nordwark virus; smoking; mad cow disease; homicidal GPs; incompetent surgeons; climate change; MS; polluted beaches; chocolate; animal rights and anti-hunt protesters; Avian 'flu; wrong diets; radio and electricity pylons; road rage; health and safety inspectors; traffic wardens; an avalanche of autocratic Euro laws … and so it goes on.

Apprehension. Fear. Both feed on memory and the *media* constantly feed our fears, encouraged by the 'Blame and Compensation culture' as it swallows taxpayers' money destined for more positive use. And, overall, there is the prevailing fear of death due to the progressive failure of Belief in and teaching of the Christian Faith: *That the grave is not the end.*

Leadership

Britain has bred great leaders who have seized their 'Golden Moment' at a time of national peril in our long, Island story, but they were exceptions.

The Times of 1st November, 2004 recorded the *jejune* views on leadership of a posse of our industrial magnates. Nowhere has this lack been more felt than in the national church from where many Church of England priests and lay people, encouraged by the leadership and example of Pope John Paul II, have returned to Roman Catholicism. The lack of missionary teaching in Church of England parishes has either ceased or, like pastoral visiting, is fast disappearing.

Santayana wrote: *"The truth is the British do not want to be well led. If they had to live under the shadow of a despotism or a masterful statesman or a deified State they would not feel free ... English genius is anti-professional, its affinities are with amateurs"*.

If Santayana is correct, it goes far to explain the electorate's neglect at the antics of the leading professional politicians who led us (traitorously, many would say) into the European Union and at the present creeping presidential style of government we seem unable to arrest.

Britain's Civil Services

But, if Britain has not bred many great national leaders, it produced in the recent past a breed of civil servants at home and abroad who have led the world in terms of their integrity, probity and sense of lawfulness and selfless service to the Monarch, to the United Kingdom, and to the peoples of our once great Empire: in fact, towards what Samuel Huntingdon would describe as 'civilisation'.

The Home Civil of yesteryear – sought by many, achieved by very few – was the anchor of the UK. Whilst the Indian Civil and Colonial Civil Services were the anchors around which those for whom they were responsible mostly thrived. Peace and order were usually sustained. The quality of life was slowly but surely enhanced. In 1975 the Vice Chancellor of Mao's 10,000-strong campus 'Institute for the Training of Minorities' could say to me: *"Times have changed. We could never govern our varied ethnic minorities as you governed India with just 1,000 incorruptibles. While until you had trained enough of the indigenous population as doctors and engineers and lawmen (as we in this campus are trying to do) you brought in your own professionals who gave their lives to spreading professional excellence, often in death-dealing climates"*. Now, thirty years after Mao's campus was founded, we see China on the verge of becoming the powerhouse of the world.

I spent five years as chairman of civil service selection boards and I certainly met some winners. But too many who passed the necessary tests seemed to me to lack the 'fizz' to which I had become used when working closely with civil servants, both as co-secretaries of two important Inquiries, or in the normal course of daily life in headquarters. One lady candidate with obviously great intellectual ability, which had taken her from one university research post to another till she was twenty-seven, came out with an answer. She saw the civil service as a 'sea of calm' compared to the work in which she had been engaged or might have to be engaged in industry or the city or the law. The civil service, she told me, would give her a quiet life and retirement security! I would not have passed her but her written work was impeccable and her psychological tests eminently favourable.

Vocation and work are indistinguishable or so it was preached to me recently by a senior churchman. I profoundly disagree. Vocation certainly implies work but work with that inner urge to sweat and labour for the common good is, to me, what constitutes a vocation and is something quite different to work. In a nutshell, I believe the archdeacon, quite inadvertently, put his finger on what has gone wrong in our Society. Vocation is OUT. Only work for money is IN.

Integrity or vocation is something difficult accurately to judge in a short three-day interview with five or six competing candidates, whilst intellect can better be measured, so the latter is apt to decide the 'Go' or 'No Go'. But the main failures in our civil service today seem to me not to be in the personnel but in the political bullying and interference and the injection of money-mad people from industry and commerce with lower standards of integrity. So all, in all, that great legacy of a vocation which I so admired in civil servants in my younger days – a wish to create a balanced political outlook for what seemed best for the Nation – has started to yield.

Yes Minister, funny though it may have been was, in fact, one of the most deadly and subversive, albeit subliminal attacks on the civil service. It has done infinite and lasting harm to the governance of Britain today.

The late Professor, The Reverend Gordon Dunstan, spoke truly in his Moorhouse Lectures[‡]: *"Behind the rhetoric of the conference room are the permanent civil servants and diplomatists ... the artificers of trust. And trust is the artefact of ethics, the keystone of all institutions built to shelter the frail but precious judgements of Mankind".*

‡ *The Artifice of Ethics,* Gordon Dunstan. SCM Press

4

Today and Tomorrow
Britain or England?

'I have seen much to hate here – much to forgive,
But in a world where England is finished and dead,
I do not wish to live.'
(The White Cliffs, Alice Duer Miller, February 13th, 1941)

I have often wondered whether I am British or English? "The idea of Britain was invented to give credibility to the Union, to sustain the Protestant religion of England and Scotland and to fortify Great Britain against continental power". So Roger Scruton quotes Hilaire Belloc. My paternal grandfather was of Huguenot extraction who found refuge in Jersey when his ancestors fled France and their vast Estates, after the revocation of the Edict of Nantes in 1685. He married my paternal grandmother the daughter of a wealthy Scottish Presbyterian Minister. My maternal grandfather came from an old Lancashire Unitarian family who married my maternal grandmother who was Welsh. So it might be said that I am truly British. But has there ever been a British nation? Jersey came with William the Conqueror, the latter's invasion force blessed by the Bishop of Caen a Le Baillif. Scots have remained determinedly Scots. Though the Welsh have provided us with the Tudor English kings, they still look on themselves as Welsh.

Only one group in our country see themselves as British – the influx of post-war immigrants. But the anti-British history of recent decades rejects this coherent idea. Roger Scruton has written: *'There was no process of nation building in the United Kingdom.'*

When I spent part of my life in a little cruiser, finally sunk after two years of constant action, with a ship's company drawn from the United Kingdom, the Commonwealth and the Colonies I often wondered what it was which triggered these men I had the responsibility of trying to lead, to show their courage and bravery and fortitude, which I found to be such a personal prop. All of them had probably left school at 14; most had little real idea of why their lives were perpetually at risk; yet somehow they sensed that what was going on in Europe under Hitler was a threat to the way of life appalling though for many of them it had been – the soup kitchen – unemployment – awful poverty – the wind and the rain and the snow as they drove the cattle in for the early morning milking. Again Scruton, I have since discovered, has put his finger on it. Somehow in their education, or deep down in their souls there was a loyalty to England: not a nation or a doctrine or a state but a **country** where we all belonged. Probably most had heard of Shakespeare but few could have quoted Richard II:

> This happy land, this little world,
> This precious stone set in the silver sea,
> … This land of such dear souls, this dear dear land.

It was England that lost many that night off Tobruk. And many like them before and after in that dark blue Mediterranean Sea.

COLLAPSE OF THE SOVIET UNION

With the disappearance in 1988/89 of the confrontation between the Western World and the Soviet Union in what became known as the Cold War, other dreadful threats to Western civilisation and our Country have emerged.

First the lowering of the West's guard has greatly encouraged the present fascistic conspiracy to create a Franco-German European Empire. An Empire in which Britain, the oldest and so far most stable democracy, would be deprived of any influence except that stemming from the views of her smallish population to the 800 million or more envisaged.

The incompetence of the economic policies set by the European Central Bank is already adding to the probability of a world recession; the interference of the European Commission with Britain's once stable society knows no bounds; the corruption within the European Union (EU) as a whole is breathtaking; EU employees are specifically above the law; EU laws to be imposed on our impotent Parliament emanate from French Revolutionary antecedents which have helped to give France no less than five different republican constitutions in the last two centuries. The EU's aggressive threat to Britain's (unique among the Nations of Europe) historic form of democracy ensures the disappearance of our Nation, its constitution, its laws, its customs and conventions and its monarchy; all these to be submerged into a number of Regions (one of them encompassing East Sussex, Northern France and Western Belgium) of an increasingly totalitarian gigantism. The future for Britain was well summed up by President Pompidou before Mr Heath came begging on his knees for entry. '*Je la veux nue.*' (I want her naked). And naked we were delivered. Our bullion rifled; our fisheries given up; our future mortgaged in almost every law, convention, feature and habits of our society.

In an International Conference at Brighton in 1978 on 'NATO and the Global Threat – What Must be Done?' I was asked by

Mr Frank Barnett, Founder of the National Strategy Information Centre and Brian Crozier, the brave Director of the Institute for the Study of Conflict, to deliver the Keynote Speech.

There was a background to this speech which I titled 'Freedom, the Fruit of Valour'. In 1971, Admiral Thomas Moorer, then Chairman of the Joint Chiefs of Staff who, when he was Chief of Naval Operations I had come to know and greatly respect when I was Naval Attaché several years before, in the preliminaries to his visit to the UK Chiefs of Staff, asked that I should brief him on the Middle East problems. Terrorism, the Intifada, the problems of Israel and the Palestinians of course took up most of what I had to say. I ended my briefing by showing a map of Char Bihar on the Arabian Sea and a chart of its then non-existent harbour (which the Hydrographer of the Navy had designed for me). I stuck my neck out and asserted that before the end of the decade the Soviets would cross the Oxus, conquer Afghanistan and Baluchistan and establish a warm-water Port on the Arabian Sea.

Most of the Chiefs of Staff, more used to my whimsies and, anyway pre-warned, calmly contemplated the always courteous comments of the Foreign Office officials. Moorer asked for 20 copies of what I had said and, six years later, when the Soviets attacked Afghanistan, wrote to recall my briefing.

It was with that small prophecy in mind, unsuccessful to the Soviets though the outcome was in the end, that in my final 'Haul Down Report' in 1975, I referred to 'the threat of Muslim Fundamentalism from the Philippines to Morocco and my belief that by the end of the century Europe would face a hostile North African shore.' That threat is now far worse than I contemplated.

At Brighton in 1978 however, the Conference was principally concerned with promulgating the imminence of the Soviet threat and although the Indonesian and the Italian delegates both agreed with me as to the Islamic threat to Europe in the longer term, our discussions were marginal, time restricted and so regrettably not fully pursued.

I believed then and I still believe now, nearly 30 years later, that there are two facets of the terrorist threat (as it has become). Conventional suicidal terrorism and the threat from Muslim Countries with weapons of mass destruction. Those two, in themselves, are only one side of the coin. The other side is the increasing apathy of the European nations, so obvious since the end of the Cold War, to renegotiate NATO into a counter-terrorism weapon. Instead, under the misdirection of those intent on a United States of Europe the emphasis has been on enlarging NATO into a more or less conventional military alliance, or preferably abolishing it altogether and substituting a multi-national European Force or armed Gendarmerie to counter civil disturbance or as a means of imposing totalitarian rule on popular opposition in their evolving fascist behemoth – (as I have elsewhere described it).

My Brighton speech concentrated on the Soviet threat. But though that military threat is now (I believe) only temporarily in abeyance, today's iconoclastic depredations of New Labour and particularly the Lib-Dems in the context of our national heritage, are precisely similar to the initial moves of communist ideology which require the destruction of all existing conventions and type of government before rebuilding in the pattern of a mythical Utopia. So I feel that it is not out of context to re-print this speech, though it was delivered at the height of the Cold War. In many ways, the perils our Nation face today are no less than that it faced in 1978 or 1940. (Appendix).

What in 1978 the Soviet Armed Forces may have lacked in quality (although in some areas of offence they were ahead of the West) they certainly made up for in quantity. The *Spetnaz* practising on precise replicas the takeover of Britain's East Coast airfields (so destroying the unique and unsinkable aircraft carrier); a two-ocean

Fleet and 400 submarines, (Hitler started with 32, half of limited endurance) most of them nuclear; three Shock armies waiting to rape their way to the North Sea; enough nuclear missiles to deter the West as the West's armoury could equally deter the Soviet nuclear threat. It was touch and go. Though today Socialist apologists accuse those who knew the facts as being 'deluded Cold War Warriors.'

In the end it was the sheer capitalist economic muscle of the West (in fact, of the United States) which could and did outpace that of Communism in the Soviet Empire and what remained of Stalin's aim of World domination. But subversion nearly undid that triumphant governmental outpouring of (mainly US) wealth that saved the World. There was little organised anti-subversive defence other than in a few patriotic newspapers, publications and the radio. Television, (as New Labour is) was iconoclastic, anxious apparently to fulfil the prime communist need, 'first destroy existing institutions and conventions which prop up society'. The non-communist influenced element of the western press remained reasonably staunch and was assisted by the efforts of perhaps a couple of dozen 'think-tanks' throughout the so-called Free World, which did much to provide influence makers with enough 'factual ammunition' to steady and inform public opinion.

Seven of these 'Think-tanks' came together in Brighton in 1978. In addition to the National Strategy Information Centre from the USA and the British Institute for the Study of Conflict there were co-sponsors from Italy, Indonesia, the Federal Republic of Germany and Turkey and 100 attendees including 60 delegates from other similar establishments in the UK, USA, Thailand, South Africa, Japan, France, Norway, Republic of Korea, The Philippines, Spain, Singapore, Belgium, The Netherlands and Portugal.

In my keynote speech, at that time of deep peril for World civilisation, and the general feeling of personal impotence to alter the flow of destiny which we all shared, I postulated the theory of 'The stone in the pond'. The pond of course was the mass of innocent busy and mainly uninformed people going about their lives as best they could, and because of the pressures of doing so, largely oblivious of the terrible threat to the freedoms and reasonable civilised society which they then enjoyed. The stone that might be thrown by such a multi-national Conference studying 'NATO and the Global Threat – What must be done?' would, we hoped, with some publicising, cause just a small ripple in the UK 'pond' (as it did). Further, we hoped that the 60 delegates who signed 'The Brighton Declaration' would be enabled to go back to their countries and cause a few more ripples which just might help to convince the public in their democracies of the very real, imminent and sinister threat to their way of life. The Brighton Declaration was not intended to move mountains; nor even little hillocks but it provided for the sixty people from fifteen countries who signed it, a small stone with which they were able to cause some ripples in the placid pond of the public opinion in their respective democracies.

In the UK today there are at least a dozen patriotic 'Movements', Institutes or 'Parties' and several great men who write for the more objective and well-informed newspapers; and these together cast stones which cause ripples of worry. But with the implosion of the Soviet Union and the euphoria of the 'Peace Dividend' the emergence of States some small, some large like Iraq and Iran, all under totalitarian rule, these sensible influences have gone relatively unnoticed or neglected. Today the West faces two threats at least as dangerous as the Soviet Union, and perhaps, because of the comparative novelty of their usage even more so. International terrorism with conventional explosives and Internet subversion is one; while the other is an array of weapons, often crude but still terrible, of various types capable of inflicting massive loss of life on people or physically damaging and perhaps leaving unusable for long periods, whole built-up areas. Such weapons are becoming available to bloodthirsty and usually irresponsible dictators.

Much of my keynote speech to the Brighton Conference was

delivered in the context of the Cold War. But on re-reading it there are parts which are as relevant today as they were years ago:

> *"Like Christianity in the past, Islam today (1978)has bred a variety of adulterated and false pieties, desecrating the true Sayings of the Prophet, and arming its misled and mistakenly adoring followers with false information and idolatrous hopes, thus causing mounting mayhem in an increasingly secular and populous world. A world tending, under the spell of television and easy communication, towards global chaos and anarchy between the 'Haves' and the increasing number of 'Have Nots' who now so easily have visible access to the life of the 'Haves'."*

5

Two Pillars of a True Democracy

LEADERSHIP

Andrew Roberts in his magisterial work, *Hitler and Churchill, Secrets of Leadership* considers leadership on a national scale. Lord Moran, Churchill's doctor throughout World War II and with trench experience of World War I has written: *"The man of character in peace is the man of courage in war"*. And with that most who have experienced a drawn-out war would agree. It was the quiet man who went on and on and on. It was the 'bullshit merchant', popular and full of go in peace, who often showed signs of cracking first.

Somewhere, I think from John Buchan's *Montrose*, I picked up the following:

Leadership

First there must be fortitude, the power of enduring when hope is gone, the power of taking upon oneself a desperate responsibility and daring all.

There must be self-forgetfulness, a willingness to let worldly interests and even reputation and honour perish, if only the task be accomplished.

The man who is concerned with his own repute will never move mountains.

There must be patience, supreme patience, under misunderstandings and setbacks and the muddles and interferences of others.

There must be resilience in defeat, a manly optimism which looks at all the facts in all their bleakness, and yet dares to hope.

There must be a sense of the eternal continuity of a great cause so that failure will not seem the end, and a man sees himself as only a part in a predestined purpose.

Leadership, then, depends primarily upon moral endowments.

LOYALTY?

Loyalty

So spake the Seraph Abdiel, faithful found
Among the faithless, faithful only he:
Among innumerable false, unmoved,
Unshaken, unseduced, unterrified
His loyalty he kept, his love, his zeal.

(Milton, *Paradise Lost*)

Anyone in a position of authority has a treble loyalty: to those in authority above him; to those over whom he has authority; and the authority of his conscience. And often there is a clash and only his conscience can decide what action is appropriate.

But in some cases loyalties can be clearly defined as in the case of the Privy Council and the European Union.

A Privy Counsellor has to swear his assent to the following:

> 'You will to your uttermost bear faith and allegiance unto the Queen's Majesty and will assist and defend all jurisdictions pre-eminences and authorities granted to Her Majesty and annexed to the Crown by Acts of Parliament or otherwise against all foreign princes, persons, prelates, states or potentates'.

Having assented to *that* oath at least three British Privy Counsellors, as Commissioners of the European Commission, have further assented to the following quite contradictory oath without in any form renouncing their previous one. Their oath to the European Union to which they have assented reads as follows:

> 'I solemnly undertake: to perform my duties in complete independence, in the general interest of the Communities.

> In carrying out my duties, neither to seek nor to take instructions from any government or body'.

In the light of these two solemn but mutually contradictory oaths, one has to ask to whom or to what do these powerful people owe their loyalty – to our Queen or to the corrupt European Commission?

Personal loyalty is surely one of the most difficult problems with which each of us has to solve. Country, family, friends, employment, political party, monarchy, church, so often there seems a clash as to where one's priorities may lie. 'For King and Country' my generation was taught – and not only those of us who went to private schools. It was the very bedrock of the teaching by men and women in the village schools, the Board schools, the Grammar schools.

LOYALTY AND PARLIAMENT

The philosophy of how different loyalties should be deployed today would take up a whole book. One in particular disturbs me greatly: the clash in Parliament between an MP's loyalty to his Party and to his Country. The first enforced by self-interest, deselection and the Whips; the second by courage, conscience and judgement.

> 'Parliament is not a congress of ambassadors from different and hostile interests, which interests each must maintain, as an agent and advocate, against other agents and advocates; but Parliament is a deliberative assembly of one nation with one interest – that of the whole; where not local purposes, not local prejudices ought to guide, but the general good, resulting from the general reason of the whole. You choose a member indeed; but when you have chosen him, he is not a member of Bristol, but he is a member of Parliament … Your representative owes you, not his industry only, but his

judgement; and he betrays, instead of serving, you if he sacrifices it to your opinion.'

(Edmund Burke. 3 November 1774)

Burke's words were surely those we boast of when we speak of Westminster 'being the Mother of Parliaments'. Today it is evident that those verities no longer apply. Parliament no longer consists of great men and women who respect the tenor of our Constitution, but of pygmies, concerned at their hours of work, the safekeeping and status of their well-paid job and their performance on television and radio. Loyalty to Party, glad-handing their constituents and repeating whatever banalities their Pager tells them to say. These are now the boundaries of their well-paid employment.

How can Parliament be described after a few years of the Blair Administration and after the much regretted retirement of Speaker Boothroyd? Kipling's description surely fits:

'Here we sit in a branchy row,
Thinking of beautiful things we know:
Dreaming of deeds that we mean to do,
All complete in a minute or two –
Something noble and grand and good,
Won by merely wishing we could.

...Jabber it quickly and all together!
Excellent! Wonderful! Once again!
Now we are talking just like men.

...By the rubbish in our wake, and the noble noise we make,
Be sure – be sure, we're going to do some splendid things.'

(Road-Song of the *Bandar-Log*)

6

The United States of America

So far these essays have dealt with some of Britain's problems. I now deal briefly with our present relationship with the United States, that Nation's developing imperium and its world role.

The terrorist attack of 9/11 2001 and perhaps even more so since, the almost simultaneous report (eventually judged to be false) that a ten-kiloton bomb of Hiroshima proportions was ready to be exploded in Manhattan shook the governance of the USA into an attitude of mind which is difficult comprehensively to describe. From it, in simplistic terms, the following defence strategy has emerged:

1. Prevention of terrorism in the United States

2. Pre-emptive destruction of terrorist nests abroad and any States creating a nuclear arsenal.

3. The world-wide spread of Western-type democratic government, if necessary by enforced regime change.

It was President Woodrow Wilson in 1919 who persuaded the West to create a League of Nations and abandon the 1648 Peace of Westphalia which regulated international order by a balance between powers and the non-interference by one country in the affairs of another. By his ideas (Wilson hoped) a League of Nations would emerge with a corpus of international law giving precedence to 'the interests of Mankind'. But the League never really survived as the powerful influence for peace Wilson hoped, largely because the American Congress vetoed American membership.

The present US government (particularly the 'neo-conservatives' in the Bush regime) have a supreme contempt for the apparently weak-kneed and overtly corrupt United Nations Secretariat (roughly the League's 1946 successor). Whilst this is understandable due to UNO's rather murky record, such a degree of contempt is not universally shared when the wide variety of problems of nearly 200 nations are, in some cases, being dealt with effectively, whilst other problems, often of extraordinary complexity are left hopelessly seeking solutions. So the US stance earns them few friends. Britain leads the few who still enjoy a relationship, albeit less happy and less influential than it was, and is often, and with reason, accurately described as the US lap dog.

It was Israel Zangwin who wrote: *"America is God's crucible, the great melting pot where the races of Europe are melting and re-forming … A fig for your feuds and vendettas. Germans and Frenchmen, Irishmen and Englishmen, Jews and Russians … into the crucible with you. God is making the American"*. It hasn't quite worked out as he prophesied. The USA today is already a 'united nation' (in 1960 the census revealed ninety-nine language groupings). Amongst the more exotic dialects were Bantu, Blackfoot, Calabrian, Concho, Coptic, Cossackian, Cree, Gypsy, Kickapoo, Kurdish Macedonian, Maori, Mon-Khmer, Nubian, Pashto, Tagalog and Chimmesyan: 500,000 people speak Yiddish and 600,000 Polish. One of the world's largest pluralistic societies flourishes despite occasional ethnic friction.

Twice in the last century Americans have been called upon to shed American blood and treasure in European squabbles from which many hoped, as emigrants, they had escaped. Further, and still within living memory, to complete the task and to bring a war-shattered Europe back to something like its former civilised state, the American taxpayer financed the great Marshall Aid plan to revive the bewildered Allies and a defeated Germany. European nations, Americans strongly believed, must now unite and stop fighting each other.

What was to become the European Union had US backing from the start. The secretive Bilderberg Conference (founded in fact in 1954 at the behest of 'The Good Nazi', Albert Speer, one of Hitler's favourite henchmen who escaped the noose due to his advice to the American team on how, most effectively to bomb Japan) funded largely by Rockefeller, has done its best to keep up a head of steam. As Chairman of the NATO Fuels and Lubricants Standardisation Committee in the late forties/early fifties, I was deeply disturbed at the clear distaste for Britain's stand in 1940 of politicians in some European nations. I knew nothing of the European Union Project then, but it was clear we were not liked and, with hindsight, it is no surprise at the price we paid for membership or that we are billed in the future to become a minor Region in a Franco-German Empire. They never wanted us in. But our dues and our fisheries provided a satisfactory entry fee for our future junior regional membership.

When there was a '9/6' and President McKinley died from an assassin's bullet (as other American Presidents have) it shocked the nation as did '9/11' some 100 years later. The then Vice President, on taking Office as President, said: *"Great privileges and great powers are ours. And heavy are the responsibilities which go with these privileges and these powers. According as we do well or ill, so shall Mankind in the future be raised up or cast down"*. George Bush rather more prosaically said much the same after '9/11'.

From Seattle to Florida, from Maine to San Diego, every morning, from primary school onwards, and including every denomination and every ethnic category, black, white, Hispanic, Asian, every American child places his or her hand on the heart and pledges allegiance to the Constitution and the Flag. In every office of every official hangs the Stars and Stripes. And it is in the DNA of every American that it is his or her duty somehow to ensure that the same sort of governance they enjoy should be shared by the rest of the world. This simplistic ethos is hammered into the fighting services in the 'Boot Camps' and at the military and civilian academies. The same theme is often voiced from the pulpit to the successive congregations who have queued outside the churches and moved forward in the sequential Sunday Services, whether Amish or Mennonite or Quaker or Anabaptist, Mormon, Pentecostal, Unitarian, Catholic, Episcopalian or the scores of other Christian denominations.

This drive for a world-wide *Utopia* is not just a policy from a Republican White House overstocked with neo-conservatives. It is an instinct in the very heart of a nation bred from a flood of immigrants escaping brutal authoritarianism. But any attempt to spread Western-type 'democracy' to all nations and different world civilisations is to stray into Cloud Cuckoo Land.

Professor Deepak Lal quotes Henry Kissinger as having sagely remarked about the attempts by (US) ethical imperialists to link trade access to China with it's human rights record: *"The proposition that freedom of speech and the press, which has never existed in five millennia of Chinese history, can be brought about through legislation by the American Congress, is laughable"*. And Deepak Lal comments: *"Such a policy can only lead to the far from inevitable clash of civilisations posited by Samuel Huntingdon"*.

Only Churchill – never Roosevelt, and none of the Allied Chiefs of Staff with the exception of Brooke – saw WWII in a politico-military framework as Stalin did. And this inability to coalesce policy between the Pentagon and the State Department at Foggy Bottom has continued and contributed to America's failure in Viet-Nam, as well as to the appalling lack of post-conflict planning for Iraq or Afghanistan.

It is clear from what has been published[§] that the unelected posse of amateur policy makers in Downing Street, who thought they knew better than those wise men in the Foreign Office and the Chiefs of Staff, and who conspired to exclude HM Ambassador from needle policy-making discussions in Washington DC, connived with the neo-conservatives surrounding George W Bush to commit that post-invasion series of fundamental errors. The price both Nations have had to pay, over and above the ballooning monetary cost, now lie in the Arlington National Cemetery and in graveyards of the United Kingdom. And it will be the same in Afghanistan.

When I lived in the States, I recall a couplet. It sums up neo-conservative policies:

All hail, thou western world. By heaven designed,
The example bright to renovate mankind.

These quick-fix modernisers on both sides of the Atlantic who want instant answers to complex problems regardless of any cost in blood and treasure, need to recall how often another old jingle has held good as the history of the world unfolds:

Faced with the Gordian knot,
Cut it if you dare,
Undo it if you can,
If you can do neither, don't despair,
The rope will rot.

In the face of profound and seemingly vexatious and intractable global changes, what the White House and the Prime Minister and the outra-

§ *DC Confidential*, Christopher Meyer. Weidenfeld and Nicholson

geous spin doctors in the Downing Street 'Ape House' lack, is *patience.*

I am a mongrel. My four grandparents were from England, Scotland, Wales and Jersey. Nevertheless, I am glad that three of my grandchildren can add America to this mixture.

Alex de Tocqueville made an extensive analysis of the American social and political system: Whether democracy in America was to survive would depend, he observed, on the American ability to survive several tests. It seems to me that these have, on the whole, been successfully met.

America has stood the trial of a terrible Civil War. Three times she has sent large armies to fight on foreign soil and since, on several occasions, lesser armed forces to do so again. To fight and to help rebuild the ravages of war she has imposed on herself an onerous burden of taxation, while in the midst of technological changes far greater than those of the Industrial Revolution. It is not, therefore, because of any doubt about her future, but rather as a reminder of the fragile nature of liberal governments and societies that Americans constantly reaffirm the philosophic view that responsibility is the foundation of freedom.

These are not just amorphous words. Surely they have a general connotation to which the whole sweep of history attests. Freedom without self-discipline is licence. Discipline without freedom is tyranny.

In our two countries today we face a common challenge. Somehow we each have to re-inoculate our dissident minorities and the too complacent majority with a national sense of direction and a faithful regard for the rights as well as the obligations, as we all make our way through life.

The dead hand of the past should not strangle the present or the future. But knowledge of what has been is a light which may illuminate the paths on which we shall have to travel in the years to come.

7

The British Empire and Commonwealth

The British Empire in India lasted for 190 years, a small episode in world history compared to the Roman Empire (985 years) or the Chinese Empire (221 BC-1912 AD) 2,133 years.

Yet in terms of numbers and power, this small island stood at the head of the greatest Empire the world has known. Its human and material resources constituted the supreme power bloc in history. None approached it in faithfulness, in international conduct, in sincere devotion to peace through justice or in the excellence of those attributes that distinguish civilisation from barbarism.

And with that Empire and a Christian background and only little Poland in support, we battled on, alone for seventeen long months, whilst the rest of a secular Europe was tumbled by or happily joined, a well-armed, vile and genocidal ideology. And so, for the second time in a single century, our last penny was spent on useless war. And many of our historic bloodlines, whether from the Liverpool 'Chum's Battalions' or Eton or Ampleforth or Glenalmond, were lost for ever in the oceans, the deserts of Africa, the Burmese jungle, Italy, France and, once more, in Flanders' Fields.

Now the Empire is no more. But our Queen is Head of a Commonwealth of fifty-four Nations and, amongst them, Monarch of fifteen Realms (something apparently forgotten by the traitorous faction who signed us into the European Union). Whilst this conglomerate is a force for good in our fractured world and must be preserved, it no longer commands the influence that the Empire once held. Indeed, were it not for the personal enthusiasm of Queen Elizabeth II and the beliefs in the Empire of some loyal Commonwealth statesmen, even the Commonwealth might not, for much longer, be held together by the silken threads of history with which it is bound.

But, somehow, it *must* be preserved for its very diversity. There is in the whole concept, a civilising strength which our increasingly fractured world increasingly needs.

8

Energy Security

In a speech to Chatham House, Dr Liam Fox exposed the extraordinary political incompetence throughout the last two decades in the handling of our future energy supplies. It was well known that existing nuclear power installations were approaching the end of their life; it was known that North Sea gas and oil were running down, so we closed our native coal mines, which still have a long life, and ceased scientific and engineering effort into the means whereby coal could be used more conveniently and environmentally friendly, as a basic energy resource.

So, by 2020, unless action is taken now and fast, we shall be at the mercy of Russia and Middle Eastern energy sources whose long-term contracts with China will limit the amount available to the UK. Our industry and exports on which our quality of life depends will be rationed and any international influence we may still possess will be lost. As an example of threats to come: Russia is charging the Ukraine $50 per 1,000 cubic metres and the EU $240!

As Dr Fox recalls, when Admiral Fisher turned the Navy from Welsh coal to oil, he stipulated that 'safety and certainty of oil supplies lie in variety and variety alone'. But Fisher's naval engineers, brought into the mainstream of naval life and future naval planning were, in the early Twenties by a backward-looking Board of Admiralty, once more sent 'below the salt' and classed as civilians whose place in the schemes of ship complements was below seamen petty officers. This became known as 'The Great Betrayal'. With no engineering representation on the naval staff able to advise what should be done, the naval requirements allowed naval boilers to be attuned to one single type of oil fuel from Abadan, the easiest to burn and not only the cheapest, but also from a company (Anglo-Persian) in which the Secretary of the Admiralty held the 'Golden Share'.

The result when Abadan oil fuel could no longer supply the Home Fleet guarding the Atlantic lifeline and taking supplies to Russia, was nearly catastrophic. Western hemisphere supplied fuels gelled in cold tanks; sprayers of fuel into the furnaces were unable to deliver efficiently; 'give-away' smoke was common; furnace brickwork collapsed. It took a major committee under Lord Geddes, with the most senior oil company representatives and the leading petroleum scientists in the UK to sort out the basic problems and guarantee a standardised supply of trouble-free oil fuel for the NATO Fleets in the post-war era.

A comparable Energy Committee of the 'very great' may or may not be in existence. But the same sort of urgent scientific/engineering priority with unlimited resources at their disposal is needed NOW, as was allocated to the development of the atom bomb in the Forties. The aim must be the same as Fisher's. *"To bring into use every variety of renewable energy including nuclear and the vast indigenous coal supplies on which we once thrived"*.

Our Energy Security, as Dr Fox so well reveals, is our 'Achilles heel'. Unless the wherewithal to ensure an adequate supply before the life span of our nuclear reactors expires, we are at the mercy of terrorists who can cut a single gas or oil pipeline or of an energy sufficient foreign government who wishes Britain ill.

9

Britain's Defence Strategy. Past and Present

Since the end of the Cold War, Britain's overall strategy (to use Churchill's phrase about Russia) *"is a riddle wrapped in a mystery inside an enigma"*. Labour, Conservative, New Labour have muddled on with little apparent forethought of where we should go or are going.

The resources needed to support our Fighting Services and the increasingly important Intelligence Services on which they rely, must come out of the same pot from which the public services of health, education, the police and fire services and the multiplying number of governmental and non-governmental bureaucratic quangos draw their fat pay cheques.

Roosevelt's action in distancing himself from Churchill and his belief that he alone could control Stalin, and Eisenhower's personal (some would say infamous) decision directly conveyed to Stalin that he would not direct the Allied Armies to Berlin, together contributed to the final strength of 'The Iron Curtain' across Europe.

This, in turn, led to the forty-four years of Cold War with its vast cost as we strove to rebuild from WWII bankruptcy. Britain's part in the Korean War added to our burden, whilst the once defeatist Nations of Europe were rebuilding fast with the vital help of American Marshal Aid.

Benelux and NATO – the Cold War

Britain was fortunate after WWII in having Ernest Bevin as Foreign Secretary. From his Treaty of Brussels and the Benelux arrangements, the North Atlantic Treaty Organisation (NATO) was born. So the Soviet Shock Armies, itching to rape their way to the North Sea, were held back by that great undertaking and the threat of the US atom bomb. And, under several aliases, designed to mislead the British electorate, what has become the European Union gradually emerged as Macmillan, urged on by Heath and Rippon, embarked on the betrayal of Britain on the absurd idea that leadership of the European Union would replace the leadership of the Commonwealth.

It would stretch this Article too far to review Britain's defence arrangements in detail between the Fifties and the Nineties. They were wholly dictated by the Cold War. Our counters to the threats, working within NATO, meant a yearly financial battle as each Service tried to ensure, within the meagre resources available, that it had the combat men and material needed if it was not to fail the Nation.

Economically, Britain was still trying to box well above her weight and it took our best post-war Defence Secretary (Denis Healey) and an equally far-seeing Chief of Defence Staff (later Marshal of the Royal Air Force, Lord Elworthy) to make the difficult decisions.

In due course we withdrew from east of Suez. A new expensive aircraft was cancelled and, thanks to a far-seeing succession of Controllers of the Navy, three Harrier/Carriers, the brain children of the great aircraft designer Sir Sidney Camm, replaced the Navy's dream of five impossibly expensive super aircraft carriers. 'The Constabulary Concept' conceived in the Sixties to curb Soviet expansion, emerged many years later as 'The Expeditionary Strategy'.

At the suggestion of Lord Mountbatten, but under the supervision of the cabinet secretary, the three Service intelligence organisations and the Directorates of Scientific and Technical Intelligence and Economic Intelligence, with the addition of an overall analysis Directorate, were combined into a six-Directorate Defence Intelligence Staff. This became the Fourth Wheel of the Joint Intelligence Committee with the DIS (civilian) Director General as the Vice Chairman of that body, an arrangement punctured by Mr Heseltine ten years later without any expressed wish for change by the chiefs of staff, and despite the acute scepticism of the House of Commons Intelligence Committee.

As General Sir Rupert Smith has made clear, the Cold War was an industry-based confrontation but the Allied (mainly American) economies could cope: the Soviet economy was hard pressed. Then the 1978-88 unsuccessful Soviet drive across the Oxus and through Afghanistan in search of a warm-water port in the Indian Ocean to help strangle the West's oil supplies was the last straw that finally broke the Soviet economy. The cost of its vast conventional forces added to the sustenance of the Soviet nuclear arsenal, coupled with the Reagan/Thatcher policies, finally achieved the economic collapse of the Soviet Empire. And we now have a united Germany and a quasi-Marxist (increasingly corrupt) Russian Federation with a large proportion of the readily-available gas and oil production within its orbit.

With the ending of the Cold War, the British electorate eagerly anticipated better days. A decade of good government under a strong prime minister had lifted the carapace of Trades Union domination. The recapture of the Falklands had boosted national morale. British manufacturing, crippled by the post-war emphasis on the Welfare State and the clouds of destruction of Britain's wealth-producing industries by poor Conservative governments (*Shipbuilding is a third World Industry* – Heath) and physically formidable but intellectually lacking Trades Union dictators were beginning to lift.

The Bilderberg Conference already referred to, saw to it that Mrs Thatcher's strength and expressed contempt for Bilderberg and the European Union was likely to delay the planned EU takeover of Britain. Wrongly believing she had the measure of them all, she allowed her Cabinet to betray her and the (Conservative) Weimar 'lookalike' under a dithering prime minister was born. Due to the incompetence of the Labour Opposition, it lasted for seven dreadful years, including membership of (and financially crippling withdrawal from) the Exchange Rate Mechanism (ERM). So Britain, once more, was at the top of a slippery slope down which, in 1997, the Country started to slide with the consequences described earlier.

The electorate happily dismissed Mr Major. In a way this was a pity as his (surprisingly competent) Chancellor, Kenneth Clarke, (a Europhile) had just brought some sanity to Britain's economic health, destroyed by the ERM catastrophe. Clarke's legacy was appreciated by his successor, Gordon Brown, who abided by it for two successful years before embarking on the traditional Labour policy of 'Tax and Spend'. Having earned a reputation as a prudent chancellor by following Clarke's policies, Brown abandoned them and, in true Soviet fashion, 44% of the electorate have now been brought onto the Labour pay roll, with promises of pensions at an early age.

10

Threats and Countermeasures

Quite unexpectedly, Dunkirk provided the greatest PR triumph this Country has known. The sight of our brave, cheerful and very battered and often bandaged Army being taken home by train, stopping at stations for tea and buns by welcoming crowds and the tales the soldiers told of the Little Ships and the Navy, reinforced by Winston's rhetoric, woke up the Nation to a degree never before (or since) achieved.

The threat today is, if possible, even more dangerous. Yet to the ordinary bloke it still seems remote. Terrorism has many facets, muggings, rape, missiles thrown from bridges at hurtling traffic, dim memories of the IRA by those close to one of its outrages, all these are more evident threats now 9/11 and the Tube bombings are becoming past history.

Yet the advances in terrorist techniques and weapons, aims, strategy and tactics over the next few years will know no bounds.

The resources are limitless; the weapons are available; the 'Causes' are multiple. Like an octopus, when one tentacle is destroyed, another will grow.

China, India, the United States and a resurgent Russia, each in its own way with the means and willpower mightily to thrive, will soon be supplying each other with the goods and services, the energy supplies, the health services to improve their standards of living. England and Europe, once the very centre of the Old World, entrenched in workers' and human rights will drop behind. The Middle East and adjacent Muslim nations will continue in a state of permanent ferment. Terrorism will be everywhere. General nuclear war with global impact will remain unlikely. Disastrous but less ubiquitous nuclear conflict will remain a dark shadow. Nuclear weapons, kept under secure control in most nations who possess them; much less in others seeking to develop them. Small 'dirty' nuclear weapons, like biological and chemical weapons, will proliferate and be at the disposal of terrorist organisations. What was the Soviet Empire is said to be still awash with ill-guarded tactical nuclear weapons.

With air travel Britain can no longer be regarded as a sea-girt fortress. Insulation from the perils of terrorist activity, already well breached, will, in practical terms, be a nigh impossible task. It will be quite impossible so long as the budding European Federation is allowed to dictate the limits of our safety nets by robbing us of the resources that even the most severe taxing Chancellor can ever amass. And the same Federation is intent on flooding England not only with immigrants, but, also, with an avalanche of mostly irrelevant, usually dictatorial laws which are turning us away from our fairly law-abiding past. The World War II 'Black Market' was child's' play compared to today's thriving fraud and 'Black Economy'.

Optimistically, and probably without consulting the swathe of anti-terrorist experts, Bush and Blair took our two countries rather deceitfully, to war, "to stifle terrorism at birth".

Unhappily, they assaulted the wrong target and succeeded only in dramatically increasing the threat. After 9/11 Bush proclaimed that the First Priority in American defence was to secure the Home Base and took wide powers to do so. When the Prime Minister and his sofa cabinet made a rather half-hearted attempt to do the same thing, they failed; probably through a lack of trust in his personal judgement in sending the country to war in Iraq. So he was unable to carry a pusillanimous parliament, most of its members unconvinced that there is a real crisis and afraid of unpopularity, refused to adopt measures to meet the real needs of Security. So our Island has remained wide open to the entry of terrorists. It is worth recalling that in 1940 thousands of innocent refugees were locked up until the situation cleared a bit and that *Habeas Corpus* was suspended. But the lack of trust is now so all-embracing that the 'Secret Sessions' of parliament held in the Forties would today have their secrets leaked within minutes.

Before listing the weapons we possess (which include the Press and TV), to confront terrorism it is relevant to recall that in the Thirties only one newspaper, the *Daily Mail* under the editorship of William Adam McWhirter, constantly supported Winston Churchill. The latter in an otherwise lonely role constantly proclaimed the perils facing our Nation in the face of a supine Conservative administration and of a Labour Opposition, just as constantly voting against rearmament.

Besides national newspapers with a feeling for the dangers ahead and, objectively, to alert the public, we have five main 'weapons' to deploy against terrorism. The Intelligence Agencies; the Police and the three Armed Services. Omitting any comments on the first of these which, it is understood are undergoing a re-hash after the government's 'Dodgy Dossier' deceit which took us to war in Iraq, there is need for long-term reconfiguration of the Armed Services and some changes in the present attitude that senior police officers have had to adopt, especially to drugs and crime.

As to the potential roles of these 'four weapons' one major point must be made clear. If we become just a number of regions in what will be the European Union or Federation and lose our monarchy, the sovereignty of parliament and our unwritten constitution as we seem set on losing, then little of what follows is likely to apply. Only if we are permitted to build our own ramparts will adequate defence against sophisticated terrorism be possible.

The Police

'A little learning is a dangerous thing' and I have only a little knowledge of the Police Service. A book given me by a great Labour Minister *The Night the Police went on Strike* and five years as a chairman of Police Promotion Boards where I was privileged to meet some of the finest young men and women our Country produces and meet and work with many of the great senior police officers of the early Eighties. Given the superlative standard of policemen in general, the mess in which the Police Service seems to be today, if the avalanche of increasing crime is any yardstick, seems to me to be incomprehensible if it were not for three clues to which I cling:

Bramshill Police College:

It may be unfair to condemn it on a one-day visit to Bramshill but, at the time, I had recently been tasked to revamp the Joint Services Staff College and I could not feel happy at the very different calibre of staff between the two Establishments. Senior police colleagues on my Boards made it very clear to me why they also felt unhappy. The Crown Prosecution Service (CPS) has lumbered the 'ordinary copper' with such a mass of administrative work that even the splendid young men I met have been overwhelmed and are no longer able to pursue crime in the manner their experience, instincts and training suggest. If there is any Body which should be 'taking up the cudgels' it should surely be the Police

College as I saw it. Unhappily, besides the low calibre staff my instincts suggested the college possessed, it now has a European role which must hinder any initiative solely devoted to ways of arresting the frightening rise of crime in Britain.

The Selection and Promotion Boards:

Besides having the benefit of the wisdom of two senior police officers as my colleagues there were certain statutory written tests which, in my view and in the view of many colleagues, favoured the better educated to those with, often, grisly and dangerous experiences as enforcers of the law. The climax came for me when two (in my view and that of my colleagues) highly gifted and widely experienced potential senior officers (from Northern Ireland) with outstanding records, clearly suffering from battle fatigue (as we reported), were turned down by the powerful psychologist authority because of their below-standard written performance. Another candidate, better book educated but, in our view, lacking the superior leadership qualities we were looking for, won through on the strength of his written work and his one recorded triumph, an efficient conviction for a hedge-side rape.

My written scream of protest (with the willing collusion of my two police colleagues) and my criticisms of several aspects of the Board psychology input and test processes were doubtless the reason why, after five years of quite hard work and much travelling, I received no more invitations (or thanks for past efforts) to Chair civil service, fire service or police service boards of any kind.

Association of Chief Police Officers (ACPO):

In the early Eighties one heard little about ACPO and its proclamations were few. Now, individual chief constables often give vent to their views on one or other of current police problems and this is sometimes, by the press, assumed to have the ACPO assent. There can be nothing wrong and much right, when these great men with their vast and various responsibilities, meet together. A lunch at Scotland Yard was one of the most animated and heartening affairs that I can still recall. But, like the chiefs of staff, unless there is a major crisis directly affecting their personal responsibility, the standing of chief constables is diminished by individuals giving press releases on single aspects and permitting ACPO authority to be quoted or assumed are out of place. In my day the Joint Intelligence committee, if challenged to give a "JIC View" always insisted that the answer should include the powerful and authoritative plural subjunctive "We". ACPO, whenever appropriate, should perhaps adopt the same custom.

Terrorism and the Armed Forces

The Army:

There can be no doubt that it is upon the Army that the primary burden of confronting terrorism at its present stage of development must fall. I do not see Britain ever again embarking on full-scale war of the Iraq type. Apart from its disastrous political consequences in the Middle East and the tragic loss of life, the war so far (December 2006) is reported to have cost the taxpayer £7B. Depending on future resources available, there may well be a case in the future as, perhaps, there was in Afghanistan, with the help of similarly-threatened allies, for dispatching well-equipped air-transported task forces to pre-empt or destroy the development of training camps and facilities and known centres of major terrorist enclaves. But there seems little or no justification for wasting precious lives and the country's wealth eradicating undesirable regimes unless invited to contribute to a UN Force legally established. So, together with such comparatively small-scale British national 'Constabulary Forces' (as General Hackett would have called them) there must be much more emphasis on Army-backed humanitarian aid. This might be on the lines of those MacArthur/Nimitz armed Construction Battalions so fundamental to the 'Island Strategy' prior to the invasion of Japan. Such air-transported forces could assist recovery after natural disasters or to prevent backward areas, for one reason or another, slipping into total chaos from which hate, genocide and terrorism can emerge.

There is also a most important Home role for the Army as the lead force to cope with any major (dirty nuclear, chemical or biological) attack. The (comparatively) minor crises during the foot and mouth epidemic showed the limits of the ability of civilian aid agencies to cope. In the event of a successful attack, Martial Law over a considerable area would at once be necessary to deal with refugees, casualties and the provision of food, shelter and medical welfare. Though the widespread physical and radioactive damage is unlikely to be on the Chernobyl scale, there will be widespread panic.

The Royal Air Force:

Like all three Services, the RAF will have several roles. I am unaware of any missile defences but the 9/11-type threat is presumably already, as far as possible, being catered for, appallingly difficult though any counters may be. But for both of the Army's overseas roles (if adopted) a massive enlargement in transport command will be necessary with the 800-1,000-seat aircraft now becoming operational. And there are arguments for some form of inter-service helicopter command observing the ubiquity of various types of helicopter platforms operated by all three Services.

The Royal Navy:

Although small, the Navy possesses a highly-trained, well-experienced submarine nuclear missile force. So long as there are nuclear-armed, so-called rogue states, who might launch a nuclear attack on Britain or on British interests or less well-armed allies, MAD (Mutually Assured Destruction) and the understanding by any aggressor that first use will be suicidal remains the ultimate and only deterrent.

When the great USN Admiral, Thomas Moorer was Chairman of the Joint Chiefs of Staff in Washington he once told me he foresaw a future where every nation with a seaboard would possess some sort of navy or maritime defence force and be responsible, if appropriate with near neighbours, for the prevention of piracy and drug running and smuggling, for a block of ocean designated by the UN.

To such duties, in the case of Britain, must be added in the future: defences against terrorists, with submarines or concealed minelayers capable of destroying or immobilising container and other vital British ports in the assault on British trade and seaborne energy supplies. Today's major cruise ships and container ships are inviting targets. This defence/offence role is admirably conducted around the US coastal waters by the US Coast guard, the second largest navy in the world

Such fundamental changes will take decades. But first the electorate have to decide.

Do they wish to become a small part of a massively corrupt European Federation, to remain in the present hotchpotch or, for a while to draw in our horns, rebuild Britain's cultural foundations in the light of a dense and changing population, before resuming a major international role?

Do they wish to give massive and scarcely monitored subventions to poorer countries?

Should we not first put our own House in order and, as far as possible, secure against the rising tide of world terrorism?

If the choice is the latter, then it can only happen if the electorate can first be brought to realise that a New Nation is being born in Britain. Further, that there will be no action unless there is a coalition of all the talents and an inter-Party Agreement for perhaps a 'New Nation' political Party, dedicated to melding the new incomers into a changing British society founded on our old verities, but certainly very different in appearance to that in which we exist today. For some decades the confrontation with international terrorism will occupy much of our system of governance and may even mean, as in World War II, putting into temporary abeyance many of those freedoms we regard as Britain's unique heritage.

11

Sovereignty or Subjection

The question facing us all is whether our Nation should retain our Monarchy, our Sovereign Parliament and our Common Law or should we yield all that has been entailed to us since The Great Charter of 1215. No political party has authority in such a matter. Only a compulsory referendum of all our people, when fully informed, can make the decision to sacrifice our past for our subjection to a Soviet-style socialist pattern of authoritarian governance or rather to build onto our existing and firm thousand-year-old democratic foundations a well-governed country at peace with itself, for the New British Nation of those as yet unborn.

Professor Scruton has written: ***"When people discard, ignore or mock the ideals which formed their national character – then they no longer exist as a People, but only as a crowd. That is happening now, in England."***

If Roger Scruton is correct, and many would attest that he is, **then any new government will have the task not only of restoring those ideals we are losing or have lost, but of merging the result with the millions flooding into the UK from all the countries of the world. These two tasks indubitably presage a New Nation.**

It is the view of this Essay that such a task could never be successfully achieved if the British parliament is inextricably shackled to the European Union. It must be that we should be "Better Off Out".

ꕤ ꕤ ꕤ

In the 1990s, George Thomas (Lord Tonypandy), one of the greatest Speakers of the House of Commons, (a Labour MP and, later as a convinced Christian, Vice Chairman of the Methodist Conference) after he had left that most honourable post, published a long letter in *The Times* under the heading: "Parliament's powers in dire danger".

A copy should be on the desk of every loyal Member of Parliament for its stark message is even truer today than it was then. ***"No political party in Britain has a mandate from the electorate to surrender our national sovereignty to foreign hands".*** Yet this is happening with the consent of a parliamentary majority but, scandalously, without the specific consent of the electorate for whom they should be speaking. Tonypandy writes of ***"subterfuges and half truths"*** and ***"how our national destiny will be subject to foreign control by a hotchpotch of European politicians who have no love for this country."***

All political parties to a varying degree, except one, stand in the dock. Hopelessly misguided Conservatives who saw in Europe a substitute for Empire, reluctantly, but mistakenly, agreed by Mrs Thatcher, too trusting of those around her already plotting her downfall (her final "No, No, No", just before they succeeded, is reminiscent of Cranmer as the flames flared around him). The

Conservatives were backed, reluctantly, by Labour (but only after Gaitskell died from a mystery illness) and, later, Labour did hold a referendum on an economic union. Such traitorous policies have been followed since by Prime Ministers and by Conservative Opposition leaders, although sometimes with weasel words of denial. We are being led by the nose into complete abrogation of our unique democratic heritage. Only the United Kingdom Independence Party (UKIP), the Democracy Movement and the Freedom Association are free from treason.

Tonypandy writes also of the special places of honour reserved for Pym and Hampden who so courageously fought for the rights of parliament against the claims of absolutism by the Crown ... ***"and of other fierce defenders of self-government by the British people, Palmerston and Pitt, Gladstone and Disraeli, Asquith, Lloyd George, Churchill, Attlee".***

Pym and Hampden's Conservative successors were reviled as 'bastards' for their refusal to vote for national betrayal at Maastricht; whilst those in UKIP who still regard the Union and the Sovereignty of Parliament to be so critical to Britain's interests that they override all purely domestic issues, have been christened 'fruitcakes' by Cameron because the votes of UKIP patriots probably lost the Conservatives 27 seats they had hoped to regain. But when sincere patriots feel as strongly as those who founded UKIP do and did, who would deny them the right to seek seats in parliament and for showing the same patriotism which inspired Pym and Hampden and of course a large part of the electorate today.

There is a difference between patriotism and nationalism or 'regionalism' or 'globalism'. ***Patriotism*** (quoting the late Pope) ***is a love for everything to do with our native land: its history, its traditions, its language, its natural features. It is a love which extends also to the works of our compatriots and the fruits of their genius. Every danger that threatens the overall good of our native land becomes an occasion to demonstrate that love.***

The native land is the common good of all citizens and as such it imposes a serious duty and loyalty.

Nationalism (or its modern larger cousins, regionalism or globalism) involves pursuing the good of a single region or of the world, with little or no regard for the enshrined rights of law and cultural heritage of each component. In plain words, Britain faces the Marxist dream of centralised sovietisation. For it was Stalin who advocated loyalty to a region as a first move to bring together continental regions into a Marxist World dictatorship.

When the Soviet Empire collapsed and, with it, what seemed to be a reduction in the volume of the Marxist message, most people were lulled into believing that was one evil disposed of. We were all wrong. A new Marxist strategy had started to evolve in about 1968, once it was clear that NATO, the early possession of the nuclear bomb by both sides and the inevitability of mutual assured destruction (MAD) would prevent the Soviet Shock Armies then exercising on the borders of Western Europe, marching to the sea and beyond.

This new strategy "Decay from Within" was well described by one of its exponents, Rudi Dutschke, when he coined the slogan which welded the romanticism of the legendary Long March of the Chinese Communists into sober and detailed Marxist tactics. It was aimed at the young and it was inaugurated in Western Germany by Andreas Baader and Ulrike Meinhof. Dutschke called it "The Long March through the Institutions".

This slow and often barely identifiable destruction of an existing society and culture and conventions was initially targeted in 1968 at (particularly) rich and mixed-up teenagers and young adults in revolt against their parents. From that source it was correctly anticipated this revolt would widen and spread, and as the older pillars supporting society crumbled (as for other reasons the Weimar republic had failed) many people would welcome a return to peace and security by a gradual rebuilding of society in a more authoritarian mode. That is what is happening.

The 'Long March Religion' was easily digestible. Further modern science, was opening up so many new avenues of information that, under the cloak of Liberalism, 'modernisation' could be so easily shown to be the obvious road forward – and the sooner the better. Without the involved doctrines of Marxism, so difficult and boring to follow, the 'Long March Religion' was something that could be preached and often innocently absorbed and then spread like a 'flu epidemic throughout the mostly unthinking world, by the many historically ignorant graduates of 'media studies' who control the media world.

And what did 'modernisation' in fact actually involve? It involved the gradual destruction of those pilot lights and signposts of religion and the law which in any way helped Mankind's instincts to separate good from bad, the God of Love from the god of evil; that interminable battle which rages within every individual. In a word, the Long March Religion seeks to instil a state of nervous breakdown, loss of confidence, fear, a general feeling of impotence: 'that it's no good kicking against the pricks' of a society decaying from within, leading to an all-embracing desire for discipline and security, however enforced. A phenomenon starting to reappear in Russia today as the freedom for which Yeltsin strove in a nation still lacking the self-discipline, destroyed in the Stalin years, creates a new demand for authoritarian security.

Whatever may be said by the opponents of the Old Labour Party, they saw in socialism a way of harnessing the industrial revolution with which Britain had led the world and moving it away from the squalor and poverty and hardship which so many (but by no means all) leaders tended to accept, as so well portrayed by Dickens and Mrs Gaskell. Methodism and other Nonconformists (Mrs Gaskell, like her husband a Unitarian) preached a more Christian quality of life for the hewers of wood and drawers of water; the child chimney sweeps; the wool and cotton spinners; the miners dying early from lung disease.

In the immediate post-war world Aneurin Bevan referred to those who did not share his view of the NHS as 'vermin'. Conservative leaders who later referred to sincere patriots in their own party as 'bastards' and in UKIP as 'fruitcakes' had much less cause to be so crudely offensive. The Attlees, Bevins, Shinwells, Morrisons, Shores, Lansburys, Gaitskells, Callaghans, Healeys, Masons and Owens were always Britons first and Socialists second. That is what counts. I always think of British Socialism in the words of Ernie Bevin, perhaps the greatest of that triple pantheon of post-war Foreign Secretaries with Alec Home and Peter Carrington (and like George Thomas, Lord Tonypandy, a strict Methodist) when he spoke at Columbia University just before the outbreak of World War II and expressed his deepest social philosophy in a single sentence: ***"We must not strive to make giants but to elevate the human race."*** A dream similar to that of Noel Wills, the founder of Rendcomb College, who gave a free education up to the age of eighteen to the children of the workers on his estates and whose philosophy still sustained in a great school was that in this modern world: ***"We need an aristocracy of brains and character".***

It was Stalin's view over the years (and Marxism does not hurry) that the first move to World government must be to a Regionalism (such as the 1917 Bolsheviks strove for by subversion) and Hitler had envisaged for Europe by conquest. Only if a degree of Regionalism could first be achieved would World hegemony be possible. Regional loyalty had to be installed as patriotism faded or was actively destroyed. That, too, was the aim of Ulrike Meinhof (herself a journalist) who with Andreas Baader were the practical founders of the Long March road to Regionalism and so, eventually it was hoped, to Stalin's type of World government.

So it is that in Britain under the cloak of old Labour Socialism, the first few miles of Dutchke's Long March has somehow created a New Labour Party – 'The New Left' which puts European Regionalism first (a typically corrupt type of Soviet-style centralisation) and our Country second with Great Britain destroyed for all time by ill-thought-out devolution. A total reversal of the priorities of the patriotic Old Labour Party.

It was a wise Cambridge Don, next to whom I once sat at dinner in his college, who warned me in 1973 of what was happening to our education system and how the French professors were combining to confront the danger. But it was not until I became Vice Chairman of the Institute for the Study of Conflict in 1976 that I realised that Professor Schapiro (the Chairman and his brave Director, Brian Crozier) with less success in our already penetrated State educational establishment, had issued the same warning some years before. No one of stature listened and the deceitful politicians of all three main parties (but primarily Heath and the Conservatives) joined the 'Long March' and betrayed Britain.

The Long March has touched all our lives in many ways since it secured power after the disastrous Major years. It has succeeded in abolishing many of those conventions governing the integrity of MPs and the lifelong adherence of oaths of loyalty to the Monarch made by incoming members of her Privy Council. Such conventions as these are now widely discarded. They needed no laws or codes or monitors. With occasional backsliders they have always been an integral part of our centuries-old unique unwritten national democratic system. To break them often incurred banishment from public life. Such is the major difference between our system of government and that of the European tribes who seek to engulf us. For them there are few conventions, only laws to be kept or constitutions to be constantly rewritten.

The New Left, or as they now call themselves, New Labour, happily treading the path set by treasonable Conservatives are in the van of the Long March: iconoclasts to a man and woman, pullers-down, *inter alia* of our parliamentary institutions now that our State education has been successfully infiltrated. They are part of the second hiccup our democracy has suffered since ***Magna Carta in 1215***. And a far more dangerous and devastating hiccup this one is proving to be. Great Britain has been brought to the very edge of the precipice and the final shove is gathering strength and almost ready.

"Come, come," Cromwell concluded his speech to Members of Parliament, ***"I will put an end to your prating. You are no parliament".*** When Mr Blair addressed his newly elected colleagues on 7 May 1997 after an hour of questions and comment, he was reported as saying: ***"Listen, it's not your job to tell us what to do."*** A few months later a top-level mole, speaking of the New Labour Millbank File to the *Sunday Times* said: ***"It is a big brother file basically. At the end of five years we should have detailed files on everybody. Very few of the new MPs have stepped out of line so far. But if there's a hint of trouble the unit is there to stamp on them."***

To 'Modernise' a favourite word of Blair and his entourage is a word with an inspiring ring. And in this changing world change is often needed. But changes in well-proven governance of an old nation must rest on firm foundations which have stood the test of time, not on newly-shovelled (and markedly reddish) sand. Yet with the Conservative legacy of betrayal well sustained, with a steady flow of immigrants of different (and differing) cultures and 70% of our laws now emanating from a source we can neither elect nor dismiss, at a cost to each of us (at present) of £100,000 per minute or £873 per person per year, this is what is happening.

We of an older generation were hoodwinked in the Thirties by the songs of the *wandervogel*, by Hitler's 'Strength through Joy policies'. We envied an apparently thriving Germany as our young in Jarrow and The Gorbals, their fathers lying in Flanders' fields or the ocean deep, stood unemployed and starving on street corners awaiting the soup kitchens. Today's escalating sleaze and deceit needs to be concealed. Just as happened in the Thirties, what is happening today is being hidden from the naive and politically innocent.

The internal combustion engine and old-type coal-fired power stations and the escalating amount of air travel may cause holes in the ozone layer and we should quickly develop answers, but sun spots are endemic. Our planet will tilt as through the millennia it has often tilted. Today's ice caps will melt; Greenland will again be green; climates will change as climates have changed throughout the ages. A blanket of green deceit is spread by all three Parties and the Greens as they mislead the media and hoodwink the electorate. After all it is only a few centuries since Edinburgh had the climate of London and London of Lourdes. And, much later, the Thames froze over. I have skied in the Cotswolds in May and within living memory Cornwall has been cut off by snow drifts.

Like the Czar and Czarina in World War I the Blairs' early years were overshadowed by a Rasputin-like figure who seems to have run Blair's sofa cabinet, told Blair what to do and, for some years, terrorised the media and created public apprehension, ably assisted by the Health and Safety Executive. When the deceit which took us to war with Iraq surfaced, he quietly left. His malign presence is reputed still to haunt No. 10 Downing Street.

In 1940 we were left to stand alone against Germany's bid for World conquest, against her eugenic policies of forced male and female bonding and the slaughter at birth of the handicapped. This hideous ideology was designed to produce a Master Race and the military conquest of a cowed and secular Europe and then the World. But by 1941 our courage and determination were not enough without arms and we became a warrior satellite of the USA.

Since, and final victory achieved, at a terrible cost of many of our best and all our wealth, we have honourably, but not always in our best interests, tried internationally to punch above our weight. The 'Marchers' constantly rubbish our historic past and archbishops apologise for the slavery Britain and the Royal Navy did more than any Nation to abolish. Under the 'Marchers' influence our old education system is being driven into collapse. With the defeat of Christian marriage we have the highest rates of crime, sexual disease and teenage pregnancies in the developed world, with diminished literacy and numeracy.

A recent Civitas Report recorded that Britain was now ***"A seriously crime-afflicted and disintegrating society ... England,***

from being a society remarkably free of crime and disorder, especially from the middle of the 19th to the middle of the 20th century, by the late 1990s had a worse record than either France, Germany or the United States."

Why else can it be that nearly four million of our best and most ambitious of childbearing couples see no hope of affording a home in Britain and so have emigrated, mostly during Old Labour and New Labour administrations? Nearly a million pensioners, many of them ex-Service people and therefore the ballast in our once stable society, have also left our shores in disgust to seek more freedom and more sun in which to end their days.

In exchange for the loss of so many of our best, New Labour 'Marchers' have deliberately, in deference to the EU, permitted immigration on a vast scale, dangerously uncontrolled in quantity and, more important, quality, making our Island, with Holland, the third most densely populated nation in the world. Whilst accepting talented foreigners of great value and golden example, New Labour has failed to exclude a mass of criminal dross to further the binge drinking, drug addiction, gambling society New Labour 'Marchers' so infamously encourage.

As the two birth rates of those who have not emigrated and these incomers diverge, the former downwards below the sustainable level, the latter, including the dross in droves, upwards, so we are becoming altogether a new sort of Nation. A New Nation is being created, possibly of great potential indeed if the explosive mix is carefully handled. There are few signs at the moment in the government or in the Opposition as to how our most critical problem of racial mix, at a time of massive terrorist threat, should be confronted and solved.

That great statesman William Gladstone once said: ***"I wish to dissipate if I can the idle dreams of those who are always telling you that the strength of England depends sometimes they say upon its prestige, sometimes they say upon extending its Empire, or upon what it possesses beyond these shores. Rely upon***

it; the strength of Great Britain ... is within the United Kingdom."

As a densely-packed multi-racial Island which can only live by exporting, and although our Queen still reigns over fifteen Realms and is Head of a great Empire, our Island society stands on the brink of chaos and disaster. The 'Long', inexorable, quasi-Marxist 'March' through our most precious institutions, parliament, education, our civil service, our presently still incomparable armed forces and, most important of all, our moral sense, has in fact been stepping out relentlessly to a drum beat from the otherwise unrecorded proceedings of Blair's sofa cabinet. And even perhaps, in part, from what Lord Turnbull has described as Gordon Brown's Stalinist propensities which, if correct, augur ill for the future.

In 1968 the centre of Washington DC went up in flames after Martin Luther King was shot on 4 April in Memphis, Tennessee. There was an assumption of a white racist conspiracy and a dread of a black uprising. Rioting, looting and burning broke out in 126 cities: 350,000 troops stood by with the National Guard to quell the riots. Terrified people clogged the streets of the capital city in a wild escape to the suburbs. There were clouds of smoke over the Potomac. The ladies on the staff of the British Navy Mission from the US Navy Building were loaded on to the seats and floor of the attaché's old Daimler for the brave Royal Marine driver to escort them to their homes. Countrywide 39 people were killed, 20,000 arrested and the damage cost at least $30 million. The attaché's wife and youngest daughter, alone and unequipped with a loaded gun as recommended (and held ready) by their American neighbour, locked the front door, with her husband's niblick close by. In any country but the United States it would have been called civil war. It could happen here.

Many people today have begun to distrust politicians. This is a pity as some are in politics selflessly to work hard for the good of the Country. It is perhaps only they (from all Parties) who now believe in the doctrine expounded by Edmund Burke (the MP for

Bristol). But with good reason, they understand that if they practise it they may be deselected or confined to the isolation ward by Party Whips.

Burke's doctrine can be summed up in his own words of a speech on 3 November 1774 in which, after his election, he gave his new constituents his definition of his duty to them as a Member of Parliament:

> ***"Parliament is not a congress of ambassadors from different and hostile interests which interests each must maintain, as an agent and advocate against other agents and advocates; but Parliament is a deliberative assembly of one nation with one interest – that of the whole: where, not local purposes, not local prejudices ought to guide, but the general good ... you choose a member indeed but when you have chosen him, he is not a member of Bristol, but he is a member of Parliament."***

For many reasons this distinction, in its strictest sense is no longer so clear-cut as even Burke found when, six years later, his constituents so resented his outspoken position on the major issues of the day that he withdrew his candidacy. For any member today this problem is even more difficult due to government interference in local affairs, particularly of education and health and local taxation. Deselection or ostracism by the Whips can ruin an MP's continued idealistic hopes for serving the Nation, his wages and pension gone. Also, too few members have known the outside world and a few have barely cut their wisdom teeth.

Parliament faces six great issues:

1) The racial impact of the imbalance between those who have left the UK and the quality of some of those who have been allowed in.
2) A massive terrorist threat, with nuclear overtones, into which more resources need to be put.
3) The breaking up of the United Kingdom by New Labour's policy of devolution.

4) The emasculation of much of our State education system by 'Long March' techniques designed to destroy discipline and abrogate teaching of the true history of our Island race.
5) New Labour's destruction of our parliamentary institution by ill-thought-out changes in the House of Lords and the time limitation of House of Commons debates.
6) The final transfer of the sovereignty of Parliament to the European Union by New Labour's 'Marchers', already partially yielded by their Conservative predecessors but now, with the apparently passive consent of the other Parties, Sovereignty is to be wholly surrendered.

Of these six great issues, it is number 6 which is the keystone in the arch and it is worth a few lines to trace the provenance of the utterly corrupt bureaucratic behemoth that now daily influences so much of our lives. Many books have charted the way in which the European Union has been allowed to take charge in a major part of our national affairs and how it is turning into an undemocratic juggernaut under Franco-Germany satrapy.

Briefly, the idealistic iron and steel community, aimed at preventing a fourth Franco-German war, later under the influence of communists such as Spinelli, coupled with the still evident German ambition to dominate Europe, was taken over by those who see the eventual possibility of a Marxist world. This aim is helped by the influence of the secretive Bilderberg Group founded by Hitler's brilliant Production Minister, Albert Speer, and his US admirers. It seeks a regional Europe with little thought of anything more. Feared by many, reviled by Lady Thatcher, despised by some British and European statesmen who, having accepted Bilderberg hospitality, found its unrecorded evening meetings not conducive to their countries' interests, unlike Heath and Rippon and Roll who were fairly constant attendees, as were many others from our parliament, industry, media and banking. More recently, a semi-secret pro-EU well-financed organisation called 'Common Purpose' has been brought into being to train up influential supporters should the EU Constitution be put once more to a Referendum.

The choice before us is plain. Do we stay in the European Union are we 'Better Off Out'?

Many believe that the latter option is the only one open to us if, once more, we are eventually to restore our self-government and again contribute our civilising democratic example to the world as Britain has done in the past, although now to an increasingly fractured world.

We have a supine parliament of whom, at a guess, 80% will obey orders, vote to stay in the European Union and betray our parliamentary sovereignty, whilst probably 80% of an electorate who, if they could ever be brought fully to understand the truth and extent of the betrayal and what it implies, would vote to leave the Union and retain our sovereignty.

The need to survive at all as a Nation is now so urgent that we must 'Pull up the drawbridge' and 'Look to our moat'. We must bring home the legions as Rome did, stop trying to punch above our present weight and boost our defences against the nuclear terrorist threat growing more deadly daily. We must leave the European Union and rebuild the proper governance of our greatly expanding New Nation as immigrants from Asia and from nearly all the nations of Europe cross our borders day by day and pack into an already overcrowded island.

So much could be accomplished given the £15 billion or more per year that we should save if we were only joined to Europe under the same arrangements as Norway or Switzerland. Those countries' European membership costs them each only a few hundred million pounds annually, and they are both thriving. That our departure would harm us economically is a transparent lie peddled by those few who refuse to face facts of the many in the world who seek our goods. And we buy more from European markets than they do from Britain. Whilst new EU laws, if we remain part of it, will so damage the City of London that it will no longer be the world's financial centre which it has so recently become. It is now possibly the main pillar on which our prosperity depends.

If we followed the Norway/Switzerland pattern, we should then be able to preserve those liberties entailed to us by Magna Carta, and by our Common Law; Trial by Jury; the Right to Silence; the rule against Double Jeopardy and, crucially important, the Presumption of Innocence and not, as proposed the European way – Guilty until proven Innocent. No longer would we be subject to laws enacted from bodies we do not elect and cannot hold to account.

Further we could regain those freedoms already arbitrarily removed by Brussels, repatriate our fisheries and grow or import our food as we wish. We could spend our taxes as the electorate may decide and not as Brussels bureaucrats dictate. Our important and widely admired intelligence assets and anti-terrorist defences liaison with other countries would be retained, whilst our borders would be for us to open or close. We could reconfigure our armed forces as we think best to safeguard the national interest.

UKIP, the Democracy Movement, the Freedom Association and a few other groupings are the only Movements or Parties not guilty of betraying our Nation. But time is too short for further argument as to the best way forward to stop the rot. Only one escape route is left us and the gate is rapidly closing. It is for the people of our Land, every single one of them in the compulsory vote, NOT Parliament who must decide our Nation's future by a referendum. All must demand that their MP should support a Referendum never to sign the new Constitution now threatening us and thereafter we must leave the European Union.

There is an abiding truth in what Mr Flea said to Mr Fly on the stomach of a bull elephant: ***"The bigger the organisation, the bigger the balls".*** The EU is a prime example. A bureaucratic socialist monstrosity, steeped in Marxism and utterly corrupt: an octopus growing another tentacle as each one is severed. We shall be 'Better Off Out'.

Again, at the end as at the beginning of this Essay, I turn to Professor Scruton for a far more sophisticated but perhaps not dissimilar view:

> "***We in Europe stand at a turning point in our history ... A process has been set in motion that would expropriate the remaining sovereignty of our parliaments and courts, that would annihilate the boundaries between our jurisdictions, that would dissolve the nationalities of Europe in a historically meaningless collectivity, united neither by language, nor by religion, nor by customs, nor by inherited sovereignty and law. We have to choose whether to go forward to that new condition, or back to the tried and familiar sovereignty of the territorial nation state."***

However, our political elite speak and behave as though there was no such choice to be made ... they speak of 'slow' or 'fast' tracks leading to a single destination – the destination of transnational government, under a common system of law, in which national loyalty will be no more significant than support for a local football team.

This Essay submits that Roger Scruton's wise words reveal in all its stark brutality, the well-hidden Stalinist ideology, reawakened by the Baader-Meinhof gang and the 'Long March' tactics described by Rudi Dutschke, all leading by the 'New Left's' process of deliberate national internal muddle and decay and thus to the establishing of Continental Regions which can eventually be brought together into a Marxist-dominated World government. This, with the aid of already perverted biological science inevitably leading to Aldous Huxley's *Brave New World* and the mass production of biological twins, ranging from the clever *Alphas* to the less well intellectually endowed *Epsilons,* and the Socialist *Utopia* of Community; Identity; Stability in a densely-populated planet.

We are in danger of forgetting, if we have not already forgotten, that we are not only heirs to a pattern of slowly-evolving democratic freedom entailed to us by those who have gone before, but that we have a duty to pass this legacy on to those as yet unborn.

So let this Essay end by recalling the last three paragraphs of Lord Tonypandy's letter to *The Times*:

> ***"For more than 600 years Speakers of the House of Commons have fiercely defended the supremacy of the Westminster Parliament. As one whose privilege it was to follow humbly in the steps of the mighty Speakers of the past, I call upon our Nation to awake, and to demand that the voice of all our people shall be heard before the next inter-governmental conference takes irrevocable decisions affecting our sovereignty.***
>
> ***A national referendum conducted before, and not after, further decisions are taken is our elementary right. This is the only sure way to prevent our parliamentary sovereignty, our judicial system, and our Commonwealth relationships from being grievously undermined.***
>
> ***We were granted a referendum on joining an economic union, but we have never had the chance to vote on sovereignty, and the issues involved, which is our democratic right."***

Signed: Tonypandy
(Speaker of the House of Commons 1976-83)

Epilogue

For reasons which are irrelevant to these essays I received, as a personal gift from the author, Vice Admiral Hyman G Rickover, US Navy, the 'father' of the nuclear-propelled submarine, an early copy of House Document No. 92-345 of the 2nd Session of the United States 92nd Congress titled *Eminent Americans, Namesakes of the Polaris Submarine Fleet.*

Perhaps more than any other engineering duo the forty-one-strong Polaris Fleet which emerged as a result of Rickover's efforts and those of Vice Admiral (Hon KBE) Levering Smith (responsible for the missiles), together with the strong Hunter-Killer nuclear submarines, did more than any other measure, diplomatic, economic, or military, eventually to bring about the Soviet Empire's dissolution. (Rickover was offered an Honorary KBE. But his determination never to be beholden to anyone or anything except his own conscience caused him to decline).

In his Preface to a series of Essays recounting the careers of those individual Americans after whom each one of the Polaris Fleet was named, Rickover concluded with these paragraphs:

> "A nation happens when people, as a result of common experience, sense a unity of interest amongst themselves and a

common pattern in their relationship, their ideas and their institutions.

Historically, in many countries, the sense of nationhood has been set by a class who felt responsible for their government. In turn, the government, being largely recruited from this group, depended on it and felt responsible for it. For much of their existence this was true of Rome and Byzantium. When this group became weakened, the foundation for support of these nations weakened and deterioration set in.

The middle class has in modern times set the national standard and tone of all Western countries. During most of the 19th century our middle class had faith in the Government and its Leaders. Their quality of honesty, dignity and identity with the Nation made that class the focal point for the deep feeling of our people for the Nation.

Today it is more important than ever that high officials and the institutions in their charge set the moral tone for our people. Contributing to this need is the lessening in religious convictions – many seeing the world as fulfilling today what in the past was promised for Heaven – and decline of the Protestant Ethic of work. If the present trend is to be arrested and corrected we must have more leaders who set the moral tone and example for our people as did men such as Washington, Adams, Jefferson, Madison, Clay, Webster, Lincoln, Theodore Roosevelt and Woodrow Wilson. Unless this takes place, we will increasingly become a fragmented Nation, each interest group attempting to use the national patrimony for its own good rather than for the Nation as a whole."

As, thanks to an unlimited immigration into our small Island, (in terms of space available needing much more packing in than was necessary in North America), who could deny that

Rickover's words do not apply a hundredfold to the New Nation we are in the process of becoming?

Our Pantheon of great men and women who have shaped us in the past is longer even than those Rickover mentions in the short history of the United States. We in Britain desperately need such people today, perhaps more than ever before. A NEW PARTY to shape a NEW NATION.

Conclusion

THE MIGHTY TASK FOR THOSE CHARGED WITH LOOKING TO OUR MOAT WILL BE TO:

- Bring home the Legions from Iraq and elsewhere. Cease discretionary wars.
- Negotiate a withdrawal from the European Union.
- Reinforce the Absolute Sovereignty of Parliament and Common Law by a House of Peers consisting of men and women selected to serve for limited periods, drawn from those already voted into the Leadership of our many great and varied institutions and the churches.
- Reaffirm and strengthen ties with all Commonwealth countries and the USA. The former group is already a notable contributor to the peace of the World. India in particular is beginning to realise the debt it owes to the 190 years of the British Raj and is becoming an invaluable force for peace in the Far East.

- Restore peace to the realm. We are a Christian country and our basic culture derives from well over a millennium of Christianity but, accepting the honourable place that Jewry already holds in Britain, the massive input of recent years requires that some form of *Concordat* has to be negotiated between the three Theistic religions, as well as with Hinduism and Buddhism, if the realm is to remain at peace within itself.
- Reconfigure the Armed Forces while retaining the nuclear deterrent within whatever resources can be made available for them and, importantly, for the intelligence services. The signposts indicating the levels of expenditure would seem to be: (1) any immediate and reliably foreseeable military or terrorist threats affecting the national interests: (2) the increasing need for international humanitarian aid: (3) the developing world situation.
- Discard multi-culturism and accept that the United Kingdom (if still united) is becoming a New Nation but a new nation still based on the existing fundamental conventions entailed to us and to the yet unborn by The Great Charter; Habeas Corpus; the Presumption of Innocence Until Proven Guilty; the existing jury system.
- Amend the Human Rights Act to include Obligations or rewrite it altogether.
- Reduce crime by enlisting locally-elected police and introducing centralized forces to deal with terrorism, drugs and other serious crimes, including major fraud.
- Introduce universal education for those, from whatever background, particularly those who are apparently gifted (at whatever age) with both brains and character or with particular skills. *"Reading maketh a full man, conference a ready man and writing an exact man"*, wrote Bacon. The aim must be to produce men and women, to whatever level they can achieve and in whatever discipline, capable of directing, or causing to be

directed, the great services of power in Nature for the use and convenience of Man, at the same time recalling that a contribution to the fall of the Roman Empire was that its education became too closely connected to the practical and its neglect of the Greek legacy of the humanities.

❀ Delegate as many appropriate elements of government as possible to Country, District or Town and Parish Councils.

※ ※ ※

Acknowledgements

For over 61 years my wife's abiding Faith and extraordinary patience, lately even with appalling sciatica, have encouraged me to bring these few essays together. At the same time she is herself publishing a book of more practical use, certainly to hard up housewives in the murky future we both foresee.

Mrs.. Freda Yates who has typed and retyped my muddle thoughts over the last few years, like me, has decided the time has come forthwith, that she too will have to cease operations. I am deeply grateful to her for her skill and patience, while concerned that my chaotic bundles of badly typed views may have hastened her decision. But Stafford will see more of her than of late. Chris Trewin and his colleagues at Trafford have equally well interpreted my suggestions about the discharge of what is probably my final shot.

The serialising of Chapter XI by that great newspaper the Western Morning News, under the skillful guidance of the executive Editor Philip Bowern, has created some differences of opinion among the paper's readership. This is what I think we both hoped; for the more people who are alerted to the way our Nations is going, with our Monarch and sovereign parliament, either at once to try to wield the same sort of world wide influence we previously enjoyed as Head of a great Empire, as many hope; or to 'draw in our horns' for a while and catch our breath, and so build up the moral and peaceful strength of the new densely packed Nation, as I advocate. This is today the critical dilemma facing the young and middle aged.

In one of his great speeches Bobby Kennedy before he was assassinated as his brother before him said this: *Each time a man stands up for an ideal, or acts to improve the lot of others, or strikes out against injustice, he sends forth a tiny ripple of hope, and crossing each other from a million different centres of energy and daring, those ripples build a current that can sweep down the mightiest walls of oppression and resistance.*

Today, some of us are coming to believe, that in the conduct of the Press and Media there are elements in both who are intent on destroying both the good and the bad that has gone before in the governance and culture and religion of our Nation. Another great American once asserted *"It is not the critic who counts, not the man who points out how the strong man stumbles, or where the doer of deeds could actually have done them better. The credit belongs to the man who is actually in the arena."*

For those professionals and others who feel that they possess more rational and enlightened minds than those of my obviously scattered wits, who have commented on what I have written with some scepticism, I commend T.S. Eliot's thoughts in 1922. These, to me, seem very applicable today.

The world turns and the world changes,
But one thing does not change.
In all of my years, one thing does not change.
However you disguise it, this thing does not change:
The perpetual struggle of Good and Evil.
Forgetful, you neglect your shrines and churches;
The men you are in these times deride
What has been done of good, you find explanations
To satisfy the rational and enlightened mind.
Second, you neglect and belittle the desert.
The desert is not remote in southern tropics,
The desert is squeezed into the tube train next to you,
The desert is in the heart of your brother.
The good man is the builder, if he builds what is good.
I will show you the things that are now being done,
And some of the things that were long ago done,
That you may take heart. Make perfect your will.
Let me show you the work of the humble. Listen.

(The Rock.)

Appendix

FREEDOM, THE FRUIT OF VALOUR

BY

VICE ADMIRAL SIR LOUIS LE BAILLY

The keynote address delivered on the opening night of the conference by Vice Admiral Sir Louis Le Bailly related the military problem to the timeless imperatives of will, belief, and moral commitment. Portions of the speech are reproduced here, in slightly edited form, as a context for the Brighton Declaration, which follows.

A British diplomat who has been drawn towards Islam … constructed what was for me a most vivid allegory. He described Ultimate Reality as being like a great mountain set in its overwhelming grandeur in a desert with no discernible end. At the foot of the mountain, in the green and fertile area around it, there are camped the nations of the world. To varying extents – depending on the clarity of their vision and how far they have climbed the mountain, and on the calibre of their guides – they are able to perceive, from a great variety of views, its great glory. Others, handicapped by faulty eyesight or mist or distance, argue in bitter disagreement about what they see. But in addition to these, there are some whose faculties are sound enough but who have turned their backs on the mountain and gaze outwards to the desert, convinced that no one can see anything more than the drab plain visible to them, and that there is no mountain, no beauty, no glory, no grandeur – nothing but empty desert.

I believe that, in truth, there are hundreds of millions of the young looking for some faith or some belief such as was furnished to an older, but much less numerous, generation by Christianity, Judaism, Islam, Hinduism, or that great counterpart to Christianity, Buddhism. I do not myself think, from the point of view of civilisation, that it matters which view of the mountain the young may choose. All these views share certain moral imperatives – certain fundamental truths and obligations on which civilisation is founded ... What does matter, I think, is that at a moment in history when technology is almost out of control, when the doubling time of the world population is down to fifty years or less, when the Earth's resources are being squandered, when European civilisation is trying to recover from two terrible civil wars, that there is this great turning away from the mountain towards the desert ...

What I seek to suggest is that certain largely unforeseen historical processes are tending to eliminate Man's natural instinct and those fundamentals of social obligation and protection, those moral conventions, by which society has lived. Further, I submit that secular law, no matter how stringently applied, can never be a substitute for moral cohesion and stability. It seems to follow, therefore, that unless we can recapture some vision, some faith – unless we "turn towards the mountain and away from the desert" – civilisation itself may be teetering on the brink of an abyss.

Alas, however, this is not the end of the matter, for we are also confronted by what one of our colleagues so rightly calls the Counter-Church. In every moral respect it is diametrically opposed to the Great Religions, and yet it has all the religious features: Messianism, absolute sacrifice, canonical texts, quasi-liturgical formulas, a creed, an infallible hierarchy, and so on. Thus, at the very moment in the sweep of history when more and more of the young are turning their backs on the mountain of Reality, beside which nothing else is entirely real, an ideology has appeared which positively encourages them to step out across the desert without a backward look.

Ask a Marxist what he wants and you will get a firm and concise answer: world revolution, the dictatorship of the proletariat, socialization of the means of production, the new man, the classless society. And even if you do not wholly swallow this Marxist cant, modern political theory seems to offer so many good things just beyond the horizon: social justice for all, prosperity for all, security for all. All of them, in this imperfect world, are mirages, such as persons see when they stumble out across an endless desert ...

In 1968, the young of the world detonated. The causes were various: Marx, Lenin, Trotsky, Che Guevara, Marcuse, Sartre, Mao, the Vietnam War, Algeria, and much else, suddenly came together into a critical mass. We saw the results in Detroit and Washington, DC, in Grosvenor Square and the Boulevard St Michel, in Japan and West Germany, and in other places too numerous to mention.

Then Russia, with the help of the Warsaw Pact, invaded Czechoslovakia. Like a bucket on a bonfire, the flames were suddenly quenched and Marxism was seen by many more for the sham it is: a highly organized system of domination of men by men; a suppression of freedom of thought, speech, and action, which is unparalleled in world history; totalitarian, bureaucratic, state capitalism at home; nationalistic imperialism abroad. But this one bucket of water was not enough – the embers still glowed. The activists have remained very effectively active, so that much ground has since been regained.

Some have turned to expressing their political credo in terms of anarchism and terror: South American guerrillas, for example, plus the Palestinian Liberation fighters, the Baader-Meinhof Gang, the Red Brigade, the IRA, and many others less overtly violent.

There is, however, another manifestation which seems to me even more dangerous: What Rudi Dutschke termed "The Long March through the Institutions." The aim of the "marchers" is clear-cut. In schools, polytechnics, universities, the Unions, theological colleges, the church, the Services, the Civil Service – in all the institutions where the young or the very young are to be found, in all the countries of what has been called "The Target Area" – the "marchers" are attempting to direct their dupes across the desert, towards the mirages of the communist Utopia ...

In addition to those engaged in the destruction of trust in our society, there is an ever greater multitude who are preparing the capability – should the Kremlin deem there to be need – for the total physical destruction by military means of the countries of the NATO Alliance ... The published evidence alone supports, unequivocally, a clear intention by the Soviet Union to establish a Total War-Winning Capability at every level of violence; and within this capability, it is the strategic missile armoury upon which all else rests. I think [most persons] would also concede that this aim is well on the way to being achieved. Soviet industry is totally harnessed to this great endeavour, and where it lacks the means, then by one way or another these means are (often willingly) supplied by the West. Additionally, grain is sold by the West to the most incompetently managed granary of its size in the world, so that the workers on the Soviet rearmament programme can be well fed ...

Few people have read these words of Winston Churchill – until recently never published – so they come to us from the grave:

> "It's no good arguing with a communist ... you can only deal with him by having superior force on your side ..."

> "The men in the Kremlin, who hold down half Europe, dread the friendship of the free civilised world ... Above all they fear the genial influences of the free and easy democratic life."

> "If they are ever convinced we are afraid of them and can be bullied into submission, then I should despair of our future … If there is to be a war of nerves, let us make sure our nerves are strong and are fortified by the deepest convictions of our hearts."

> "Let us beware that foolish visionaries do not sap the pillars upon which our country stands and destroy our families, our homes and our happiness."

So now, coolly, let us examine the circumstances in which this vast Soviet military juggernaut might march. There seem to be to be four main points:

1. To what degree, as judged by the Kremlin, has the spiritual destruction of The Target Area proceeded? How far has "The Long March through the Institutions" gone? How many of the young have been turned to the desert?

2. To what extent are the pressures mounting against the regimes in the satellite countries? In assessing this, the Kremlin will no doubt consider the pressures from their own brave dissidents.

3. What of the Empire? Has what Professor Seton-Watson calls "The Law of Colonial Ingratitude" (something familiar to one or two from nations here tonight) become significant?

4. How dominant will the younger military be under Brezhnev's successor?

… Brezhnev's policy, as I interpret it, has been to establish a firm base camp from which the final spiritual assault can be made – by stepping up subversion and the threat of physical assault – on the peak called Western Europe. The Politburo must see that the problems endemic in the world are helping "the continuing struggle."

All may yet go well, without a nuclear exchange, if the Soviets display …

- ❁ Patience at the top
- ❁ Coercion at home, among the satellites and in the Empire
- ❁ Subversion abroad in the uncommitted world
- ❁ Subversion and military blackmail against The Target Area

Patience, Coercion, Subversion, and Military Blackmail – these are their main weapons.

Therefore, if we allow ourselves to, as we say in the Navy, "let go the end," the Soviet assault by subversion will go forward in fine weather; and by the early 1980s, the final peak will be scaled and Europe will be Red. But if we make the going rough – if we constantly and publicly proclaim the truth of what is happening, if we transmit across the walls by every means open to us the ideas and beliefs of the liberal democracies, if we at the same time fortify ourselves against terrorism and nuclear blackmail – then rest assured that the subverted and the faint-hearted, those who constantly "decline the danger of war," will do their best, as indeed, they are doing this very week, to create panic and hysteria and the belief that if we do not lay down our arms we shall be dead. We shall need, in Winston Churchill's words: "strong nerves fortified by the deepest convictions of our hearts" – but I believe that if we do this, and only if we do this, the final assault may be delayed indefinitely and our children will live in freedom …

The greatest difficulty, as we sit here at Brighton, is not to develop a sense of utter futility – the feeling that alone we cannot do anything to cure the World's distemper. Surely, however, there is something in the "stone in the pool" theory. Each time a stone is cast the ripples spread out and a little bit of the encroaching bank is washed away. The bigger the stone, the bigger the ripples and the faster they work.

We must proclaim that the whole concept of pluralist democracy is disappearing from the world as Marxism-Leninism and its mutations … by coercion and intimidation plunge nation after nation into a totalitarian night. We must proclaim that each time one of us yields individually to the totalitarian spell, or fails to stand up and be counted, as at times I am afraid we all do, then one battle for civilisation is lost …

Our future may be beyond our vision, but it is not yet quite beyond our control. Ladies and Gentlemen, instead of planning another conference, can we not at this one carve out a large stone? …

It is so easy to preach, and I would not so do unless I was prepared to practice what I preach. So with Brian Crozier's help, I have prepared a small stone ["The Brighton Declaration"] which you may feel is suitable, after amendments, to cast into the smooth pond of Western complaisance and constant retreat. We might publish it in our daily papers, for example, for all to read.

It may not produce many great ripples, but surely, Ladies and Gentlemen, it is only those who dare to fail greatly who can ever achieve greatly.

THE BRIGHTON DECLARATION

The Brighton Declaration was signed by more than sixty participants at the Brighton Conference.

Meeting together in conference at Brighton, we the citizens of a diversity of nations share a common concern for the defence and security of the non-communist world. We agree that what is at stake is not only sovereignty and territorial integrity, but the preservation of a way of life. It is common ground between us that the threat, in this broader sense, is now greater than ever before – and is still growing. In this belief, we call on each of our governments:

TO PROCLAIM the nature of the threat posed by the "continuing struggle" of the Union of Soviet Socialist Republics to spread its totalitarian system to all the countries of the world, and to make known not only the dimensions of the mighty Soviet military forces but also the extent of the attack on the non-communist world by subversion, disinformation, psychological war, support for terrorism and the denial or endangering of the supply of essential raw materials and energy.

TO ESTABLISH AND SUSTAIN among the non-communist nations a capacity and common policy for counteraction against this mainly non-military attack.

TO LINK détente and Soviet access to non-communist technology and other services and products, including wheat, more rigidly to substantive Soviet force reductions and greater respect by the USSR for the spirit of the Final Act of Helsinki 1975, especially in the free flow of people and information between East and West.

TO INCREASE popular participation in the aims and spirit of the North Atlantic Treaty by establishing a NATO Assembly integral to that organization.

TO ACKNOWLEDGE that the dimensions of the threat have now spread worldwide and that, as a consequence, all the nations of the non-communist world must become more closely involved in confronting the threat.

TO WORK positively and actively for greater cohesion, stability, and trust within and between the nations of the non-communist world, so that our united strength, common sense of values, and concern for the future of Mankind may become more evident to those under totalitarian thrall. Thus we may help to sustain them as they strive so valiantly to replace the tyranny under which they suffer by some pluralist system of democracy of their own choice.

www.ingramcontent.com/pod-product-compliance
Ingram Content Group UK Ltd.
Pitfield, Milton Keynes, MK11 3LW, UK
UKHW041846190726
13854UKWH00002B/741